WILLIAM R. STEELE

Presentation Skills 201

*How to Take it to
the Next Level as a
CONFIDENT,
ENGAGING
PRESENTER*

**Outskirts Press, Inc.
Denver, Colorado**

Presentation Skills 201:
How to Take it to the Next Level as a Confident, Engaging Presenter

Outskirts Press, Inc.
http://www.outskirtspress.com

ISBN: 978-1-4327-3840-2

Outskirts Press and the "OP" logo are trademarks belonging to Outskirts Press, Inc.

PRINTED IN THE UNITED STATES OF AMERICA

Contents

        Commit to Planning✓

        Define Success ?

        Make Sure It Has a Theme

        Remind Yourself: You're Not the Audience

        Break Out of the Box

        Don't Ignore the Small Voice ?

        Don't Prepare "More Than Enough" ✓

        Include Stories ✓

        Inject Humor but Don't Try To Be Funny

        Build Understanding with Examples

        Work in a Prop

        Answer the "So What?"

        State the Obvious

        Start Strong, End Strong

        Provide Internal Summaries

        Transition with Questions

        Fight Off Last-Minute Changes

        Give Yourself the Best Stage

        Craft Your Message First, Then Your Slides

        Make Your Visuals for the Audience

        Plan to Go Without a Slide

        Be Visual With Visuals

        Navigate the Slide Deck Smoothly

        Don't Fall Victim to the Technology

        Take Ownership of Corporate Slide Presentations

Preface

Most people who sign up for a presentation skills workshop need improvement. Otherwise, they would not take the time away from their busy schedules.

Occasionally, however, exceptionally strong presenters show up in a class.

Ask them why they are there, and the answer is amazingly consistent. They are looking for "one more thing" they can do better as a presenter. Seeking improvement when they no longer *need* it has become the key to their high performance.

You could say they have a Toyota attitude toward presenting.

In recent years, Toyota has been challenging General Motors for the title of Biggest Automobile Manufacturer in the World. General Motors has held this unofficial title for over half a century. Most people would have thought GM's hold on the throne was permanent.

How did Toyota grow so dramatically?

Most business analysts would say the answer lies in Toyota's corporate culture—a culture built around an obsession with continuous, incremental improvement. Its employees constantly look for one more thing they can do better.

Like the people at Toyota, presenters who rise above all other speakers are the ones who are always looking for one more thing they can do better. Their commitment to incremental improvement leads to exceptional skills.

But why make presentation skills a priority?

Let's face it; most people just want to survive their public speaking responsibilities. *I just want to get through it without messing up or having a nervous breakdown.* To them presentation skills are survival skills. The only potential they recognize is potential embarrassment.

In reality, presentation skills have enormous potential to advance a career. Influential, senior leaders are most likely to be in the room—ready to be impressed—when someone is presenting. The positive impression of a strong performance can pay off big down the road.

This truth was underlined at a presentation skills class I once conducted. The corporate vice president who had scheduled the workshop gave some opening remarks. He told the class participants that he had arranged for this training because he wanted them all to become vice presidents. However, if this was going to happen, they needed to know how vice presidents were selected.

He explained that the senior decision makers cannot make a final promotion decision based on resumes alone. Typically, they find themselves with three or four final candidates who are equally impressive "on paper" (range of experience, education, positions held, etc.). When that happens they have to shift their focus to the "impressions" they have of these people. And these impressions, he declared, are often based on the handful of times the candidates presented to them.

Each presentation became a "snapshot" of the future candidate, this VP explained. Then, declaring, "This is you to them," he pantomimed the animation of several still shots by fanning an imaginary stack of photos.

Strong presentation skills build careers. When it counts, they leave long-lasting impressions of someone who can confidently and professionally handle a high-pressure situation that demands clear thinking and clear communication.

But I don't have time for more training!

Unfortunately, the high-performing professionals who most appreciate the need to hone their presentation skills have the least amount of time for training. They're too busy attending meetings and giving presentations!

I wrote this book for these professionals. The ones who have said to me over the years, "Just give me something I can do right away to take it up a notch." They want actionable ideas that generate immediate improvement.

Does this describe you? Are you committed to continuous improvement as a presenter? Are you always looking for one more thing you can do that will make you a more effective speaker? If so, this book is for you.

In the pages that follow you will find over 70 tips that have proven themselves over and over in the 16 years I've been coaching presenters. Implement just a few of them and you will see significant, career-building improvement in your presentations. Implement many of them and you *will* stand out from the crowd when critical impressions are being made.

Let me stress, this is **not** a step-by-step guide to creating and delivering presentations. There are hundreds of books that meet that need. I titled it *Presentation Skills 201* because I expect you, the reader, to already be a competent presenter. The information in this book is for enhancing your skills.

Start at the beginning and read to the end, or jump around to points that interest you. Keep the book in your desk drawer as a reference guide. If you implement one new idea each time you present, the cumulative improvement will put you at the top of your game.

1
Planning

Commit to Planning

I regularly meet good presenters who are unlikely to ever become great presenters.

They have talent, brains, and knowledge. They are comfortable with public speaking. They have no trouble expressing themselves. Words come easy.

People who hear them present are always complimentary. *He does a nice job. She expresses herself well and comes across with a lot of confidence.*

What keeps them from becoming great speakers is that they can't bring themselves to plan their messages. *I'm best when I just go up there and start talking. If I plan too much* ("too much" being defined as hardly any at all) *I don't do well. I get all tangled up in what I am supposed to say, instead of just saying it.*

Their idea of planning a presentation is to "put together a few slides" at the last minute. If they are part of a presentation team, they assure the rest of the team that there is no need to go over their portion of the presentation. *I'll be fine. Just tell me what you want me to cover and I'll look it over on the plane.*

Are they dodging work? Some are. Many, however, really do feel smoother in their delivery when they minimize planning. They *have* had trouble with structured pieces and they *have* experienced being more comfortable when they didn't "think about it too much in advance."

Unfortunately, these presenters consistently trade away the difference between good and great in exchange for an easy sense of flow. The words come easy, but there are too many words. The message flows, but it becomes repetitious. Interesting points get made, but don't get fully developed.

If it sounds like I'm describing you, please reconsider the value of planning. You will always do well enough "just talking," but that next step up to great presentations will elude you. Great presentations take planning and polishing.

The spontaneity you prefer needs to be on the other side of preparation. In other words, you need to craft your message, practice it until it's refined and you own it, *then* you can push your notes aside and "just talk." What will make it special is that it is *not* just talk: It is a well-thought-out, carefully crafted message.

Peter Hall, former director of England's National Theatre, says: "You have to have the discipline and then you will be liberated by it."

Chapter 1 Planning

When you have had the discipline to plan well, you can take liberties in your delivery and still have those great lines, engaging stories, and consistent focus that characterize an exceptional presentation.

The first tip for immediate improvement: Stop the "I'm best when I just get up there and talk" business! You will only really be *best* when you start planning what you are going to say.

Define Success

I was once asked to coach the head of an American manufacturer that had just been acquired by a European conglomerate. The new parent company had decided to fly sales managers from throughout the world to America for a meeting at the new subsidiary. The purpose of the meeting was to familiarize these managers with the product line of the subsidiary and encourage them to sell these products when they returned to their home countries.

My assignment was to get the American executive ready for a presentation that would kick off a day of site tours and demonstrations. He wanted to put special focus on a cutting-edge product his company had just developed. When I asked him what he wanted to accomplish with this presentation, his answer was "Impress them."

What do you think of that as an objective? Does it sound a bit vague to you? It is.

How are we going to determine if they were impressed? A few nods? A few smiles? A handful of compliments?

Even if we do somehow determine that they were impressed, where does that leave us? When they head back to the airport, what tangible results will we be able to point to?

I pushed this gentleman to come up with a concrete result he wanted from his presentation. I asked him to define success. He ultimately decided that a few pilot programs would constitute success. *If they will go back to their country and get a customer to agree to a pilot program, I will cover all costs. I just need a chance to prove the product.*

That was good. Now we had something concrete to shoot for. But, when I asked him how many pilot programs he wanted, he became angry. *What do you mean 'how many do I want?'* Obviously, he hadn't given it any consideration and also didn't want a measurable goal. Eventually he settled down and defined success as four pilot programs.

Now that success had been clearly defined, we were able to strengthen the presentation with a pilot program module and a clear call-to-action. The final results were double his goal: eight pilot programs. As I watched him high-five his fellow American executives, I could only think: Had we not defined success, we would not have achieved success.

Never be vague about what you want to accomplish with a presentation. The old adage holds: If you don't know where you are going, you will end up somewhere else.

Define success. Define it in concrete terms.

Chapter 1 Planning

Make Sure It Has a Theme

In his book *Lend Me Your Ears*, William Safire features 200 of the best speeches in Western history. He has several criteria for judging a speech, and the one he calls the "single most important ingredient" is *theme*. A speech cannot be good without a clearly identifiable theme.

What is a theme? According to the American Heritage Dictionary it is "a topic of discourse or discussion," or "an implicit or recurrent idea."

Safire makes this concept easy to understand. He urges speakers to consider what audience members will say, after the speech, if they are asked what it was about. If they can answer that question in "a word, a phrase, or a sentence," the speech had clear theme.

Safire is talking about speeches, but this same acid test should be applied to any presentation you are planning. What will audience members say afterward if they are asked what your presentation was about? Will they be able to summarize in "a word, a phrase, or a sentence?"

We have all sat through presentations that wander all over the place. The speaker talks about one thing for a while, and then switches over to something else unrelated. If we are asked later what it was about we don't even attempt a good description. *Nothing special, he just went over a bunch of stuff about procedures and budget issues.*

Start making *theme* an essential ingredient of all your presentations. Before you put together your content ask yourself: "What do I hope audience members will say if they are asked what my presentation was about?" Decide what you want the word, phrase, or sentence to be; then build your presentation so that it stays consistently focused on that theme.

If interesting, but unrelated material suggests itself, leave it out. If you are tempted to make the presentation do double duty—*as long as I have them in the room*—fight the temptation. Make your predetermined theme the acid test for judging all possible content.

After you present, no one should have trouble answering the question: What was that all about?

Remind Yourself: You're Not the Audience

You put the final touches on a presentation, step back, and declare, "It is good!"

It came together nicely. It flows well. The audience will love it. Right?

Maybe. Maybe not.

A sales manager I know has changed how she interviews potential salespeople. She has begun asking them to describe the last significant purchase they made. She has learned that people tend to sell the way they buy. (Example: A person who analyzes comparative data when buying stresses comparative data when selling.) A candid story about a purchase gives her valuable insight into their selling approach—an insight she would not get from rehearsed answers about selling.

This idea that people sell as if they are selling to themselves also applies to presenting. People present as if they are presenting to themselves. It's the natural thing to do.

The problem, of course, is that the audience in a presentation may be quite different than the speaker. It may include people who have different priorities, needs, attitudes, preconceptions, backgrounds, training, cultural orientation, and learning style preferences. Their judgment of the presentation could be quite different than the speaker's.

The speaker may value in-depth detail, but the audience wants a quick, "bottom-line" report.

The speaker is concerned about strategy issues, but the audience needs tactical solutions.

The speaker's understanding of the subject is highly advanced, but the audience is being exposed to it for the first time.

I once worked with an industrial chemist who provided a perfect example of a speaker preparing to speak to himself instead of his audience. I was charged with getting him ready to brief his company's senior management on a new product being developed. I listened to his presentation and could barely understand it. I felt like I had stumbled into an advanced chemistry class.

When he finished, I asked him about the senior executives he would be speaking to. Did they have chemistry backgrounds? No, they did not. They were all from the business side. *That's why they are flying me in. They need to get up to speed on the chemistry.*

I asked what happened the last time he presented to them. From the look on his face I could tell it was not a good memory. He eventually admitted that they had started reading their mail while he was talking. Simply put: He lost them. They could not follow his message and gave up trying.

Were these executives dumb people? Of course not. They were smart enough to run a global company. They simply were not chemists. They did not understand what he was saying, and their needs were not being met, so they mentally checked out.

It must have been frustrating for everyone involved. I'm sure this chemist worked hard to create the best possible presentation. After all, he was getting a chance to impress the "higher ups." The problem was not a lack of hard work. The problem was that he automatically, unconsciously, assumed that what impressed him would impress them.

Of course it didn't help that he also found these executives intimidating. He naturally gravitated to his source of confidence: his chemistry.

We rebuilt his new presentation based on the priorities and backgrounds of the senior executives. It was a struggle. The result did not meet his personal standards for scientific rigor. It did, however, please the audience. They left their mail unopened and concentrated on what he was saying. He held their attention and succeeded as a communicator.

The next time you prepare a presentation, keep repeating to yourself: "This is not for me; it's for my audience. This is not for me; it's for my audience." Keep putting yourself in the shoes of the people you will be talking to. What will best address *their* needs and *their* wants? What will hold *their* attention and be meaningful to *them?*

We all gravitate toward the same thing: a presentation we would want to hear.

We're far more likely to be successful if we craft what our audience members will appreciate.

Break Out of the Box

I was fortunate with my first job in the business world. I worked for an executive who was willing to take the time to mentor me.

To my great benefit, he would regularly set aside time to teach me something new and share his wisdom. At the time, I didn't realize how rare and special this was. I was a class of one in a graduate-level business course—and didn't even know it.

One piece of advice, in particular, captured my attention. It permanently lodged in my mind:

"If you want to get ahead, you have to be willing to do what others are not willing to do."

When the consensus around you is "That's not necessary," or "That's enough," you have to be the one who makes the extra effort, does the "unnecessary" thing.

He explained that most people stick to the accepted norm. They follow the pack.

I learned years later that this tendency is part of something called the principle of social proof. In his book *Influence, The Psychology of Persuasion*, Robert B. Cialdini, PhD explains that this principle refers to the strong tendency all humans have to judge what appropriate behavior is by observing what others are doing.

Most of the time, living by this principle is a good idea. We save ourselves a lot of time, energy, and grief by taking cues from others.

There is, however, a downside. The principle of social proof can also keep us from breaking out of the pack when we should. Challenged to do something different, something creative, we back away, telling ourselves that "no one else is doing it."

Did you ever wonder why so much advertising is the same? During several years in the advertising business I learned that most clients want creativity until you give it to them. Faced with approving an advertising campaign that would make them stand out as different, they suddenly don't want to be different. They opt instead for something similar to what everybody else in their industry is doing.

I run into this mind-set all the time when coaching corporate presenters. Instead of saying, "No one else is doing it," they will give it the official sound of quasi-policy: "That's not how it's done here," or "That's not how they want it done." If I suggest something that would enhance their presentation, their knee-jerk resistance begins with "You need to under-stand how things are done here." Somehow I am supposed to help them stand out while simultaneously being careful not to make them stand out!

The strength of this stick-with-the-norm belief was evident in a workshop I taught a few years ago. A young marketing executive, who had just recently given her first presentation to senior management, described how she had invited the CEO to participate in a demonstration. As she enthusiastically described this part of her presentation there was an audible gasp in the room. Mouths hung open. No one could believe that she had done such a thing. "You had the CEO do what?!?"

It was sad to see the expression on her face change from excitement to worry. Up to that point she had been so proud of that presentation. Now, you could hear a confused defensiveness in her voice as she described how willing and complimentary the CEO had been. I could not help but think, *She'll never do that again.* She will learn to observe what the others do and fashion her efforts accordingly. Fearing group censure, she will not stray outside the box again.

The point is *not* that she should always do demonstrations and invite senior management participation. It was appropriate in that presentation. It may not be appropriate again for quite a while.

The point is that she creatively enhanced her presentation with something that made an important point in a memorable fashion. In the blur of presentations senior management sat through that week, hers made an impression. She worked outside the box, too new to the culture to even know there was a box.

When you get ready to deliver a presentation, ask yourself: "What would give this piece extra impact? Invoke interest? Make it memorable?"

What you come up with may not follow the norm. And, of course, it won't be necessary. But it just may save your presentation from being forgotten before it's finished.

TGR versus TGW

Years ago I listened to an audio recording of Tom Peters' book *The Tom Peters Seminar*. One segment in particular jumped out at me. Although it was about quality control in the automobile business, I could see a direct application to presenting.

Peters explained that Detroit significantly improved the quality of its cars by focusing on a statistical measure called TGW (**T**hings **G**one **W**rong). An emphasis was put on driving down the TGW count per hundred vehicles produced. The lower the TGW count, the higher the quality.

He then went on to talk about how the Japanese made a conceptual leap ahead of the Americans by shifting their focus to *miryokuteki hinshitsu*: TGR (**T**hings **G**one **R**ight). With this focus, they concentrate on enhancing the experience their cars give. They work on what it will take to make their cars truly special. Nothing is too small, even the feel of the radio knobs. As Peters likes to put it, the overall goal is a "Wow!" response from consumers.

Closer to the business of presenting, Peters applies this principle to the theatre. He asks his readers if they have seen a great play lately. Then he asks if it was great because the actors didn't make any mistakes. Of course not! It was how engaging they made it, not how error-free. Imagine yourself saying: "Boy wasn't that wonderful! None of the actors flubbed a line."

As I said in the introduction of this book, too many presenters just try to avoid making mistakes. Success is defined as getting through a presentation without messing up. If they recognize any potential, it's the potential to fail.

Each time you go to the front of the room, you have the potential to stand out and make a strong impression. You have the potential to wake people up, capture their imaginations, change their minds, and move them to action.

The key is going to be your willingness to break out of the box. It's going to take a shift from minimizing TGW to increasing TGR—an effort that Tom Peters says "takes unadulterated flair."

Don't Ignore the Small Voice

With this segment it may sound like I am immediately pulling back from my advice in "Break Out of the Box." That's not my intent. I only want to make you aware of a challenge you will face when striving for creativity.

Sometimes when you are brainstorming creative ideas, a small voice in the back of your head will sound a warning. *That may not be a good idea. People will misunderstand.*

At times this is the voice of convention, a voice that *should* be challenged. At other times, however, it is the voice of wisdom, a voice that *needs* to be respected. Your success depends on sorting out which it is.

As I emphasized in "Break Out of the Box," you will have more impact as a speaker if you push the boundaries of your comfort zone and actively keep yourself out of ruts. At the same time, you have to value your experience and trust your instincts. These two imperatives can sometimes seem like they are in direct opposition to each other. There is a dynamic tension between the two that you have to manage without killing either one.

I mentioned earlier that much advertising is bland because advertisers nervously stick with what everybody else is doing. When I was in the advertising business, an advertising agency in the Northwest was having notable success avoiding blandness. Its founders became anointed gurus. People wanted to know how they succeeded in creating so many creative campaigns. One of the agency's founders was fond of saying that you were not on the right track with your thinking unless it made the client nervous. If the client was uneasy, then you were potentially on to something. Whatever you were doing, it had the potential to get attention.

There is a lot of truth in that advice. Safe ideas that feel comfortable to everyone rarely stand out. This holds true in presentations as well as in advertising. A few raised eyebrows in your audience may be just what you need to differentiate yourself and your ideas.

That said, pay attention to your own uneasy feelings before you create those feelings in others. When that small voice in your head says be careful, respect it. Intuition is not given the credit it deserves.

If I am unsure of something—a story, a prop, a piece of humor—I'll let it percolate in my mind for a while. I'll leave it in my notes with a check next to it and see how I feel about it the next day. If I still like the potential, I'll take it the next step and practice it. How does that humor sound when I actually say it? Does that "cool" idea of a demo actually work when I integrate it into the presentation?

Often, that small voice that was warning me to watch out quiets down after revisions and polishing. I gain confidence in the idea and go with it.

Other times, the red warning light keeps flashing. If I go with the idea, then I'm probably going to regret it. *Boy, that didn't go over well.*

I've learned to be particularly leery of highly emotional content. It can give a speech or presentation extra impact, but it can also be surprisingly difficult to deliver. Even when you get comfortable with it in practice, you have to be careful. On the day of the real speech or presentation, the anxiety of public speaking is going to meet up with the emotion of the story, and the combination may be too much. I've watched speakers unexpectedly overwhelmed by their own emotional content. They struggle to get back on track.

Be creative. Take risks. But respect the small voice of intuition.

Don't Prepare "More Than Enough"

"More than enough" is good. Right? More than enough money is good. More than enough time is good. More than enough gas in the car is good.

Most presenters will tell you that having more than enough material is good. *I'm all set. I have more than enough.* The stack of notes is thick. The slide file is huge. Everything has been graphed. Every bullet point has sub-points. *I've got it covered.*

Please! As you pull together your content, don't set out to have more than enough.

Effective presenting is about effective communication. This means the *outcome* is more important than the *output.*

Success is not measured by how much you cover, but by how much your audience understands, absorbs, and, if appropriate, acts on.

Years ago I had a coworker who was responsible for creating new-business proposals. He would joke about the "thud factor." With tongue-in-cheek he would judge how impressive a written proposal was by how loud of a thud it made when dropped on a conference table. He was joking, but something equivalent to the thud factor drives many presenters. They believe more has to be better. It's not!

If there were Laws of Presenting equivalent to the Laws of Physics, one of those laws would declare an inverse relationship between effective communication and content tonnage. This "law" would say that there is a point at which the more you say, the less you communicate.

As a presenter pumps out more and more information, the level of effective communication begins to slide. Instead of leading to enlightenment, the 200th bullet point produces glazed eyes. Eventually, effective communication falls off to zero. The audience stops paying attention. *I'll just read this stuff later. Maybe.*

Chapter 1 Planning

Some presenters are motivated by fear. They don't want to be accused of not covering everything. *What if they point out that I didn't include a particular competitor in my analysis?* Others believe it takes a lot of information to be persuasive. *I need to show them that I've covered every angle.*

But the number one reason presenters load up with too much material is a simple fear of running out of things to say.

I've asked scores of workshop participants if they have ever actually witnessed someone running out of material too soon. Few can think of anybody. If they do remember an early end to a presentation, it is a fond memory.

You need time for quality.

By keeping the material tonnage down, you can fit in more stories, examples, and audience participation. These ingredients enhance a presentation, but they are time consuming. Sadly, presenters routinely leave them out in favor of more slides.

In addition to engaging content, you want to be able to take the time to fully develop ideas, emphasize points, and pause regularly. In other words, you need time to work the material.

You Want to Own the Time

One of the keys to sounding confident as a presenter is acting like you own the time. If you were told you have 15 minutes to speak, you want to act like you own those 15 minutes.

Rushing makes you sound anxious to the audience. It undermines the confident image you want to project. You risk coming across like a nervous stage performer who expects the hook at any moment.

Limiting your content takes the pressure off.

Anticipate the Senior Executive Hurry-Up

For presentations in front of senior management add one more step to your limited material: anti-rush preparation.

Unless you are scheduled to be the first presenter, assume the time slot you have on the agenda is not worth the paper it's written on. It might say 10:00-11:00 a.m., but it's going to end up being 11:40-Noon—if you're lucky. Everybody before you is going to run long, eating away at your share of the meeting.

You don't need a crystal ball. You know the routine. As you go to the front of the room, the person in charge is going to tap his or her watch and urge you to cut it short. *We're running behind, Susan. Can you give us the short version?*

The typical presenter interprets short version to mean fast version. Do not make that mistake! Actually create a short version in advance. Call it your Executive Version. The full presentation might be 30 slides long, but this version has just the eight or ten you absolutely need to make your main point. If someone wants to see the other slides, they can be made available in hardcopy.

Without the pressure to cram all your slides into a short-ened time slot, you can maintain a confident pace *and* avoid getting cut off. The poise you show will be worth its weight in gold—particularly when you are in front of the kind of people it pays to impress.

Chapter 1 Planning

The next time you are tempted to prepare more than enough, remember, more than enough is too much.

Include Stories

People love stories.

They sit in an audience, marginally paying attention to a presentation, and then they hear words that wake them up: "Let me tell you about an experience I recently had." Or, "Just the other day I was talking to one of our clients and…"

When a speaker transitions into something anecdotal, there is this sense that something is being brought to life; a concept is becoming more real and understandable; our ability to relate to the message is being given a boost.

Stories involve an audience in a unique way.

In his book *The Springboard: How Storytelling Ignites Action in Knowledge-Era Organizations*, Stephen Denning describes his research into why storytelling is such an effective communication tool. He found that audiences drop their intellectual guard when a speaker starts a story. After all, how dangerous can a story be?

Also, Denning explains that audience members "co-create" stories. In other words, they add to the story with their own mental pictures of the participants and settings. This co-creation results in the audience members taking ownership of the story. This explains why the only thing you can remember weeks after a speech or presentation is the story the speaker told. That was the part of the message you co-created in your mind.

If a story communicates the essence of your message, it's especially effective. The essential point you wanted the audience members to remember is lodged in their minds.

It may be a silly example, but recently I learned how a point I made to someone over 20 years ago has stuck with him because of the story I told. This gentleman worked for me when he was relatively new in the business world. At some point we talked about business dinners, and the advice I gave him included a warning about ordering meals that defy graceful eating. I made my point with a story about the disaster I had when I ordered a sloppy meal during my first important business dinner. When I exchanged e-mails with him recently he mentioned that he still tells that story. I didn't ask, but I will bet he also still watches what he orders at business dinners.

Stories are also invaluable for conveying an idea or vision that is not yet fully fleshed out. For example, a business leader who is attempting to turn a company around may see that poor cooperation between departments is a problem. Maybe, given six months of committee work, it would be possible to roll out a highly detailed integration plan. But, the company doesn't have the luxury of time. And even then, no plan could be counted on to anticipate every possible situation in a corporate-wide effort. If the leader tells a story that captures the essence of what good cooperation looks like, the employees will work out how to bring it about in the scores of individual situations they face.

When I recommend stories, I'm not recommending novel-length narratives. You're not sitting around a campfire keeping people entertained for hours. In presentations—versus speeches—stories are not lengthy parables; they are typically anecdotes. The American Heritage Dictionary defines an anecdote as "a *short* account of an interesting or humorous incident." What is "short"? Think of your story as a slide-length component of your message. It's not written out on a slide, but the time it takes you to tell it is roughly the amount of time you would typically take to go through one of your slides.

Collect stories. Don't wait until you are putting together a presentation to try to remember a relevant anecdote. As you experience or hear about something that might make an interesting ingredient in a future presentation, jot it down somewhere. The first step toward including memorable stories in your presentations is remembering them yourself. Until they are put in the context of a message they can be lost.

As I said at the start, people love stories. They're waiting to hear you say: "Let me tell you about an experience I once had."

Inject Humor but Don't Try to Be Funny

At the beginning of every presentation skills workshop, I listen to the participants talk about their learning priorities. What aspects of their presentation skills do they want to work on and improve? One of the priorities I hear all the time is "I want to be funny. I want to inject humor into my presentations."

I understand completely. Speakers who can make an audience laugh are popular. It's the most frequently cited reason people give for liking a speaker. *Oh, it was wonderful. She was so funny.*

And it is not just about being popular. If you have ever succeeded in getting an audience to laugh, you know how great it feels. In a matter of two seconds you can go from being a nervous wreck to feeling like the whole world loves you. Seeing the smiling faces; hearing the laughs; it's a tonic for the soul.

And, if that's not enough, laughter can open people up to be more receptive to a message. Some of the most powerful speakers I know have a style that gets people to lower their guard through laughter and then hits them with a profound thought or a sobering challenge. Then, just as they feel the audience becoming too weighted down by the heaviness of the message, they lighten it up again with something funny. If you look at their speech or presentation in its entirety, you will see a consistent pattern: laughter, strong message, laughter, strong message. It's very effective.

With all these benefits, you would expect me to recommend that all speakers work at being funny. I'd like to, but I hesitate. I've witnessed too many speakers fail when they try to "crack 'em up." They go for laughs and nothing happens. They try again, and still nothing. They laugh at their own stuff and nobody laughs with them. Finally, to make sure the situation is truly awkward, they comment on the humorless atmosphere and blame the audience for it. *Boy, this is a tough crowd. I'm going to have to get some new jokes before I come here again.*

Some people are simply not good at being funny. Their timing may be off. Or, what they think will be unexpected—a key component in much humor—is not. Or, they can't navigate the tricky currents of political correctness.

Chapter 1 Planning

Typically I advise people to avoid trying to be funny if they know it's not their forte. It's downright painful to watch someone trying hard and failing. They don't call it "dying on stage" for nothing.

Instead of trying to be funny, think more in terms of light humor. Instead of trying to generate loud laughter, shoot for smiles. Ideally, you want to set up the possibility of some laughter, but not the need for it. In other words, if nobody laughs, it's not a big deal. You can just keep moving along on your message without leaving the impression that something has fallen flat.

I have a rule for myself: The audience laughs first. I'll say something that I believe is humorous, but I won't smile or laugh unless audience members react first with smiles or laughs. That way I never get caught chuckling—alone—at my own material. If no one reacts, I just move along to my next point. *Was I trying to be funny? I wasn't trying to be funny.*

This rule has served me well. I have learned that there are no guaranteed lines. I can say something that has consistently generated laughs, and the audience I'm currently talking to will show no reaction. Who knows why it didn't work? As long as I don't demonstrate that I was expecting a laugh, I'm fine.

This need to avoid obvious failure is the main reason you want to stay away from jokes. Jokes declare themselves. You might as well say: "This is supposed to be funny, so get ready to laugh." It's either going to succeed or fail. You can't just move on as if laughter wasn't the objective.

Also with jokes there is the minefield of political correctness. Today so many people are looking for a possible offense, it's difficult to know in advance if a joke is safe. You might think it was harmless only to learn that someone was "terribly offended." I was reminded of how strong PC has become in recent years when I watched a "Best of Johnny Carson" DVD. One of his guest comedians in the 1960s "brought the house down" with a joke that would cause a serious incident today.

The safest humor revolves around experiences you have had. Something personal and anecdotal adds color to a message even if it doesn't leave them rolling in the aisles. It also doesn't depend on a punch line and has the validity of being something real that you experienced.

If you want to keep it real safe, consider poking light fun at yourself. You don't want to jeopardize your credibility by being too self-deprecating, but showing yourself to be human can both generate smiles and strengthen your personal connection with the audience.

In the end, if you keep it light and don't try to be a stand-up comic, you can reap the benefit of humor without getting the hook.

Build Understanding with Examples

"Let me give you an example." It's a line audience members love to hear. It generates a wave of relief when they need a better understanding of what is being presented.

A concept that is as clear as day to you, can be as clear as mud to people hearing it for the first time. A simple example is often all it takes to enlighten them. *Okay. I get it. I see what you're saying.*

A business manager, *for example*, may be presenting a new customer service initiative dubbed "Customer Advocacy." Smart audience members are going to generally grasp the idea. But, if they hear an example of someone acting as a customer advocate, their understanding will instantly increase.

Sometimes examples are not just helpful, they're critical. Audience members can misinterpret what is being said if they don't hear an example. A human resource manager may promote "vacation policy flexibility" only to find employees taking unintended liberties. *What do you mean I can't automatically extend my vacation if I'm having a good time? I thought you said our policy was flexible.*

The main resistance to giving examples that I run into is that presenters are reluctant to be specific. They feel that an example may cause their listeners to think too narrowly about the message. *I don't want to give them a specific example because then they won't consider other possibilities.* Wanting their audience members to "run with the idea," they risk leaving them stalled at the starting line.

Omitting examples is not how you avoid limited thinking. You encourage people to "run with the idea" by using *multiple* examples that span a range of possibilities. Typically it takes only two examples that are markedly different from one another. The audience members get double help understanding the concept, while getting the message that there are any number of ways the concept can be applied.

Whenever you find yourself wondering if an example would help, assume it would.

Work in a Prop

Props get attention. In a presentation world of two-dimensional visuals (read: slides), props come across like something that jumped off the screen, into the middle of the room.

An audience can be riveted by something as simple as a partial glass of water that a speaker holds up as part of a talk on being optimistic (seeing the glass half full) instead of pessimistic (seeing the glass half empty). The glass isn't necessary, but it enhances the speaker's effectiveness by bringing the concept more to life.

The use of props is so rare that any presenter using one is almost guaranteed extra audience attention. In fact, audience members will start asking about a prop when they first walk into the room and see one sitting on a table or standing in a corner. I just recently helped some doctors get ready to do knee injection workshops, which incorporate model knees. One of their constant challenges is getting their workshop participants to pull away from the model knees long enough for the initial slide presentation.

In one of the most effective presentations I ever delivered I used poker chips to drive home a budget message. I was charged with getting several marketing directors to stop depleting their budgets before the fourth quarter. They had heard this message in previous management conferences but had never changed their behavior. I was determined to break through.

Chapter 1 Planning

As the marketing directors were taking their seats, I pushed a table into the center of the room and spread out a long sheet of paper divided into 12 squares. I then stacked a large quantity of poker chips next to it. As you can well imagine my preparations generated immediate attention. *What in the world is he doing? Something tells me this is not going to be a typical presentation.*

In my presentation I started walking through a hypothetical marketing program. With each square on the sheet representing a month of the year, I piled my "budget chips" where they would be needed to pay for the advertising, promotions, and special events I wanted to do. I purposely used examples that people in my audience had actually done in the past. Each new example generated nervous laughter somewhere in the room.

Do you want to guess how many chips I had left when I reached the last couple of months of the year? I left myself with just two and then had some fun with a melodramatic cry of dismay. *How am I going to make it through the holidays? I've burned up all my chips!* At this point everybody in the room was smiling and laughing.

I paused for the laughter to die down and then I switched to a serious tone. *Do you recognize yourself in this demonstration? Have you burned up your chips in the past? Have you left yourself without the resources you need to run a successful fourth quarter?*

Not only did my use of props breathe new life into a chronically ignored message, it helped me generate change in behavior. In the subsequent 12 months I would hear one report after another of marketing directors carefully preserving funds for strong fourth-quarter efforts. In fact, "burning off your chips" became part of the corporate lingo. I experienced the highest level of success—changed behavior—and the poker chips were a big part of it.

In addition to visually enhancing a presentation, a prop can also appeal to the tactile needs of some audience members. There are people who just have to touch a product before it becomes real to them. These are the people who could not imagine buying a piece of clothing off the Internet or out of a catalog. They must go to the store and feel the fabric.

If I was recommending the change to a new piece of portable equipment because it weighed less than the current equipment, I would have to consider having one available for audience members to hold. Sure, I could probably get away with just detailing the weight comparison on a slide, but somebody—maybe a key decision maker—would respond more favorably after actually holding the lighter product.

I'm not recommending that you pass something around the room while presenting. Then your prop becomes a distraction. Either have it available for inspection at the end of the presentation or stop presenting long enough for the few people in a small audience to handle it.

However you ultimately use a prop, the increased audience attention you generate will be obvious. You will have broken out of the two-dimensional world most presenters inhabit and generated three-dimensional impact.

Chapter 1 Planning

Answer the "So What?"

Good salespeople are selling all the time. They roll out of bed and start selling their kids on eating breakfast. Before they finish their first coffee they begin selling their spouse on weekend plans. Within minutes of arriving at the office they are making a case for some new program.

If you were to follow them around, you would hear them constantly stressing the benefits other people will derive from doing what the salesperson is proposing. You would hear them telling the kids that eating breakfast will give them energy. You would hear the spouse being told a day at the beach will be a great stress reliever. You would hear the boss being told that a new program will increase market share.

These salespeople live by the old adage "Features tell; benefits sell." If they want you to sign up for some kind of service, they don't just say it comes with a money-back guarantee (a feature). They describe how this guarantee eliminates any worry about having to pay for unsatisfactory results (a benefit).

It's not that they think you are incapable of working this out for yourself. They simply know that they have a better chance of persuading you if they actually state the benefit. They understand the importance of not assuming you will think about it on your own.

I am constantly meeting people who are not in sales, but desperately want to be more persuasive. They need budget approvals, permission to hire people, changes in job responsibilities, and the cooperation of customers and coworkers. Yet they deliver their presentations and nothing happens. Or, if something does happen, it's not what they wanted.

Why do they fail to persuade?

They fail because they do a lot of telling without selling. They tell, and tell, and tell about what they are proposing, but they don't stress the benefits to their audiences. They operate with the assumption that their listeners just need the facts, and then they will make "an informed decision." In other words, they assume the people they are presenting to will work out for themselves what the benefits are.

You can never assume that your audience members will recognize the benefits of what you are proposing. No matter how obvious you think these benefits are, you have to communicate them. *But I shouldn't have to spell it out to them!* Oh, yes, you do. *But I'll be insulting their intelligence.* No, you won't. They will naturally accept the benefit statements as a legitimate part of your message. You would only risk insulting their intelligence if you overdid it with a particular benefit and became a broken record.

The last time my wife and I bought a computer, I noticed just how many features can be emphasized without benefits being mentioned. Every company advertisement or Web site I looked at included a long list of product features without a word about why I should care. Whether it was about the size of the screen or the processing power, I—apparently—was supposed to know what the benefits were. Fortunately, my wife has a great deal of computer experience, so she explained the benefits. In other words, she had to take on the responsibility of persuading me. I assume all these computer ads are written by computer people who can't imagine having to "spell it out." They believe that an impressively long list of features is all that is necessary. Wrong.

Chapter 1 Planning

One of my fellow trainers introduced me to a simple exercise designed to teach the difference between features and benefits. It involves passing a bottle of water around a roomful of workshop participants and having each one of them identify a feature of the bottle and explain the benefit of that feature. If they say, for example, that the bottle is plastic (a feature), they have to go on to say why plastic is a benefit (it will not break if dropped). This exercise does a great job of bringing alive the "features tell; benefits sell" concept. Try it yourself. See how many feature-with-benefit statements you can come up with. (Hint: You can repeat a feature if you can think of a different benefit.)

I follow up this exercise by telling workshop participants that they should envision cartoon-like thought bubbles above the heads of their audience members. In these thought bubbles they should see the question "So what?" Every time they talk about a feature of their product, service, or plan, they should immediately envision everyone thinking, "So what?" The key to delivering a persuasive message is to keep answering the "So what?" question.

If you tell a group that your proposed plan includes more teleconferences and fewer in-person meetings, imagine them thinking, "So what?" Then, without waiting for anyone to actually verbalize this question, answer it. *This will cut down on your travel and the amount of time you have to be away from home.*

Every time you deliver a presentation, be committed to answering the "So what?" question. Your persuasiveness will increase dramatically.

One last thought: Make sure you stress benefits that are

valuable to your audience members, not benefits that are more important to you. They don't want to hear how much better your life will become; they want to hear how much better *their* lives will become. "If you agree to this it will lighten my workload" is not a good benefit statement.

I once worked with a sales group that made signs that said "So what?" and attached them to sticks. People in the audience would hold them up whenever a presenter gave a feature without a benefit. The next time you practice a presentation, you may want to tape your own sign to the wall.

State the Obvious

I want to briefly expand on a point I made in the last segment (*Answer the "So What?"*). That point is that you have to state the obvious when presenting.

When you were a kid you would hear things like: "Do I have to spell it out for you?" Adults wanted you to "think it through" and "work it out for yourself." That kind of training taught you to "use your head"—which is good—but it also made you leery of saying anything to others that might be considered too obvious. You learned early that you didn't want anyone saying, "I know. I know. You don't have to tell me."

The challenge you have as a presenter is that everyone in your audience does not necessarily see what you think is obvious. Some may not make the connection at all. They are the ones who later say things like "Oh, that's right. I didn't think of that." Others come to conclusions you never intended. *That's not the way I took it.*

For example, you might be speaking to a management group about a growing problem with customer satisfaction. You have processed the results of several customer surveys and now you are taking the managers through a series of slides summarizing these results. It is obvious to you that automated systems have made the customer experience too impersonal. In fact, it's so obvious *to you*, that you assume it's obvious to your audience. But, later on, you find out that the key decision makers left your presentation believing that the automated systems have to be made more user-friendly. *No. No. No. The customers don't want a better automated system; they want to talk to a human being!* The point that was obvious to them was obviously different than the point that was obvious to you.

One of the axioms in formal logic says that if *A* equals *B*, and *B* equals *C*, then *A* equals *C*. It doesn't get much more obvious than that, but the axiom isn't complete until you state *A* equals *C*.

When presenting, state the obvious. Then your message is complete.

Start Strong, End Strong

Not all the parts of a presentation are created equal. The beginning and the end have an extra potential to be noticed.

People tend to remember first and last impressions. These tendencies are referred to respectively as the primacy effect and the recency effect.

Given these "effects," it just makes sense to start *and* end strong. In other words, make a *meaningful* impression when an impression is likely to be made.

"That makes sense," you say. And yet presenters typically put little thought into their introductions and conclusions. In fact, even careful planners will start and end with unplanned comments. They labor over the body of their presentation, spending hours getting the slides just right, and then trust they'll adequately start and finish with spontaneous, off-the-top-of-their-head comments.

Are these comments eloquent? Rarely. On the front end, they come close to babble. *So how is everybody doing? Good? Good. I really appreciate you taking the time for this—even if it did take some donuts to get you here. Ha. Ha.*

The conclusion—if there even is one—sounds like an afterthought. *So, aahh, thanks for coming. Hope you, aahh, got something out of it. Call me if you have any more questions.*

The front-end babble comes from a combination of nerves and no specific plan for what to say first. The urge is to say something—anything—just to "get settled." The typical result is the kind of meaningless chat you hear when uncomfortable strangers first meet. Far preferable would be a planned and practiced opening that can be relied on *despite* the nerves.

Poor endings are the result of neglect. Presenters work out what they will say on their last content slide and then they assume the question & answer period will take care of the rest. They see no compelling reason to plan what they will say after the last question. After all, that's essentially the end of the presentation, right? No, it's not.

Chapter 1 Planning

Starting Strong

When you first face an audience, you are looking at people preoccupied by all sorts of things: the conversation they've been having with the person sitting next to them; the presentation that preceded yours; the work piling up back at their office; their weekend plans... etcetera, etcetera.

You need to get their attention and make a good first impression of yourself and your message. The old saying that you never get a second chance to make a first impression holds with presentations.

Ask yourself, "What can I start with that will compel these people to turn their attention to me?" It needs to be something relevant to your topic that will effectively launch you into it with everybody on board.

It doesn't have to be something dramatic or funny. You're not trying to win an Oscar or be a stand-up comic. Your objective is to get the audience tuned in and anticipating the message.

You have any number of choices.

You can start with a thought-provoking statement. *I don't know if you are aware of this, but in the next five years our market is projected to triple in size.*

You can begin anecdotally. *I'd like to start out by telling you about a conversation I recently had with one of our biggest customers.*

You can poll the audience. *By a show of hands, how many of you have run short of product samples in the last month?* One rule about this approach: You have to process the results of your poll. *Just what I expected, the majority of you have. Today I want to talk to you about possible solutions.*

There is no Best Way to Start. A thought-provoking statistic may work well for one presentation, while a series of polling questions is better for another. I have to admit that I favor anecdotal starts when I present. People love stories and I like to take advantage of that. I also find that I feel most confident in those initial nervous moments if I have an interesting anecdote. Personal stories are least likely to fall victim to memory lapses.

From now on, make sure all your presentations start out with something attention-getting that makes a good, strong first impression. Go straight to it without babble.

Ending Strong

Who controlled the ending to your last presentation?

If it ended with you answering a question, the person who asked that question controlled the ending.

This makes the last question and answer subject to the recency effect. The audience is more likely to remember this exchange than other parts of the presentation. Just think of all the kinds of questions that could make for an unfavorable final impression. What if the last question is hostile? Or, what if it is totally irrelevant and leaves the audience thinking about the wrong issue? It may even be a question you can't answer, so the presentation ends on a display of your ignorance.

If you let your presentation end on a question, you are ceding control of your ending to the last questioner. You're allowing this person to decide what the rest of the audience will hear last. Don't do that. It's your presentation; you should control how it ends.

Keep an eye on your time and finish up with questions while there is still a minute to make your PLANNED final remarks. *Thank you for your questions. While we still have a minute I would like to wrap up. I will stay afterwards for any additional questions.*

If you have some housekeeping matters to cover, do them first. *There are some extra handouts in the back if anyone needs one. I stapled my business card to them. Feel free to e-mail me with any questions you have later.* Then close out with a statement that delivers what you want remembered most. You can lead into it by saying, "If you don't remember anything else about this presentation, please remember this."

Later, when audience members think about your presentation, or are asked what it was all about, your closing statement will be what comes to mind.

In personal relationships, being someone who always has to have the last word is not a good thing. However, being a presenter who always has to have the last word *is* a good thing.

Provide Internal Summaries

When a presentation gets long, your audience members need help. They need help keeping everything straight. You can provide this help by occasionally reviewing what has been covered so far.

Reviews that take place in the body of a presentation are referred to as internal summaries. Typically, they occur at the end of major sections in the presentation. *Before we go on to the next section in my talk, let me briefly review what we have covered so far.*

These internal summaries can be accompanied by a reappearance of the main agenda slide. Each time it comes up, the section just finished is highlighted while the speaker reviews the main points covered. Then the next section is highlighted as a lead-in to the new material. I like this approach because it repeatedly gives the audience members a visual reminder of the overall structure of the presentation.

Internal summaries can also be accompanied by questions from the audience. This approach is a nice compromise between taking questions all the time and making people hold them until the very end of the presentation. Constant questions can make time management difficult in a long presentation, but few people will hold on to a question about something that was covered 30 minutes earlier. Reviewing key points and taking questions while they are fresh is an effective way to reinforce the foundation you want to build on in the next section of your presentation.

Transition with Questions

In order to maintain the consistent narrative that every good presentation has, you need to transition smoothly from one slide to the next. You don't want a break in your flow. The idea is to have a continuous, overall message, not a series of separate slide messages.

An interesting experiment that will tell you if you are transitioning well is to have someone else advance your slides when you are rehearsing. If you are effectively setting up the next slide and talking your way into it, your slide helper will know when to advance by listening to your message. If you have to keep saying, "Next slide please," it's a good indication that your slide transitions need some work.

If you have trouble working out a transition, you may have to change the slides. But, before you do that, try this fix. See if you can transition to the next slide by posing a rhetorical question that the next slide answers.

So as you can see, we are experiencing chronic delivery problems with raw materials coming from overseas suppliers. Why is this happening? Let me take you through the primary reasons we have identified. The next slide then is the answer to the "Why is this happening?" question.

I saw how helpful this technique can be when I was working with a product manager last year. He was finding it particularly hard to come up with slide transitions. It didn't help that someone else had created the presentation and he had been asked to limit his changes. Once I showed him the technique of transitioning with questions, his problems were over. He was able to quickly tie the slides together and eliminate the breaks in narrative that had been plaguing him.

Fight Off Last-Minute Changes

There comes a point in the run-up to a presentation when no more significant changes should be made. Practice has become more valuable than any change—unless it is to repair a mistake or fill in a glaring omission.

But I just want to add a couple of slides and beef up the budget section. No! Don't do it!

You will be more successful with a well-rehearsed "B-grade" presentation than an "A-grade" presentation that has not been adequately rehearsed *in its entirety.*

A presentation is not like a stage set that can be made better by last-minute changes to the lighting. A presentation is the actual play. The "actors" must be fully rehearsed. If they are not fully rehearsed because of last-minute rewrites, their lack of fluency will take more away from the performance than the new content added.

You are going to be particularly susceptible to last-minute rewriting if you are either a procrastinator or a perfectionist. For procrastinators, last-minute rewrites are actually necessary editing that should have been done days ago. For perfectionists, changes are the wrinkles in their dress that are making them late for the wedding rehearsal.

One other thing will make you susceptible: a micro-managing boss. It makes me nuts how often I have readied an individual or team for a big presentation, only to learn that the boss was making changes an hour before the meeting. It's either arrogance or ignorance to believe these changes are so valuable they warrant potentially undermining what a lot of hard work and practice have honed.

Determine in advance when you need to stop making changes in order to have time for practice. Then, when you reach this point, have the discipline to stop tinkering and rehearse what you have. Politics and power may limit what you can do about the boss, but make every reasonable effort to head off those last-minute changes. When the presentation goes well, even the boss will be satisfied with what you put together.

Give Yourself the Best Stage

I once found myself teaching a two-day workshop at a company that had laid off a large number of people the day before I arrived. Some of the people in the class were last-minute substitutes for people who had been let go. Understandably, the atmosphere was tense.

During the first day of the workshop, my class members told me that senior management had scheduled a meeting for that evening. Everyone was expected to attend. I would need to wrap up my teaching 30 minutes early so that they could get over to the main building.

I could only imagine the hard work the senior managers were putting into preparing their talks. After all, this was a pivotal moment in the history of the company. A failure to shore up confidence and reinforce morale could lead to a crippling "brain drain." Essential people would head for the exits.

At a point in the class when we were talking about how to arrange a presentation room, I asked my class to describe where senior management would be speaking to them. I learned that it was a large room created by opening a portable wall separating two adjacent rooms. We discussed the wisdom of using such a large room given the absence of so many laid-off workers. It was agreed that this would not be a good idea. Empty space would emphasize the company's trouble.

Unfortunately, the senior managers did not think about the room. I'm sure they were preoccupied with what they were going to say. While they prepared and practiced, the maintenance crew set up enough seating for the pre-layoff crowd.

You should have heard the sarcasm when my class returned the next morning. *Oh sure, we're doing just great. The future is bright. No reason any of us have to worry about losing our jobs.*

Too late to do anything about it, the senior managers had shown up to a room with rows of empty seats. And, of course, these empty seats were right up front. It didn't matter how optimistic their message was, the visual message of loss overwhelmed their vocal assurances. It would not be too harsh to say that the presentation was a failure.

This was a dramatic example of how the physical setup for a presentation can affect the presentation. Usually, it's not so obvious. Yet it is always a mistake to dismiss the importance of room setup.

Poor lighting, background noise, blocked views, uncomfortable temperatures, too much room, too little room—these "small" things have a way of undermining the attentiveness and receptiveness of an audience.

Chapter 1 Planning

Give yourself the best possible stage. Make logistical planning an important part of your preparation process. Fifteen minutes making sure everyone will be able to see the screen can have more positive impact than 30 minutes fussing with the design of a slide.

I know if you are like me you don't want to be a bother. *Oh, I'm sure it will be fine. We'll make do.* Let a facilities person act the least bit annoyed, and the temptation is to immediately back off. *On second thought, just leave it the way it is. If they have trouble seeing the slides, I'll ask them to move their seats. If they can't hear, they can move forward.*

Of course you don't want to turn into the presenter equivalent of a demanding rock star or diva. However, you also don't want to see your success jeopardized by an environment that could have been better. Be *reasonably* firm about what you and your audience need. The right setup can be the edge you need.

If you're presenting as part of a large event, changes can be hard to make at the last minute. Talk to the event coordinators in advance. Tell them what you need from them in order to succeed. They may stubbornly insist on their way of doing things, but don't be put off. After all, you are the one going up in front of the audience, not them. It doesn't hurt to remind them of this sometimes.

When I think of the stubborn resistance of support people, I think of this one marketing executive I coached. He was preparing to speak at a sales meeting and needed to do something about his reputation for being a stiff, overly formal presenter. I had him rehearse getting out from behind the lectern and down closer to the audience. We also worked in some audience participation that would require the house-lights to be up so he could see the audience members.

During the meeting break before his slot on the agenda, I asked the lighting guy in the back of the auditorium to turn up the houselights. He wouldn't do it. He had been keeping the lights off for slide shows all of his professional life and he wasn't going to change now. Fortunately my client was a senior executive and was able to go over and order the lights on.

His get-down-close-to-the-audience performance was excellent. Later, he was told by one of his associates that his "new style of presenting" was "fantastic."

This success would not have been possible if he had not insisted on the right environment.

Let me take this opportunity to say a bit more about this lighting business. Years ago the lights in a room had to be turned off in order for the overhead transparences or slides to be seen. Projector lights were weak. Today, projection units are so powerful your slides can easily be seen with the room lights left on. Yet, the tradition of turning off lights lives on. Day in and day out, presenters forfeit the opportunity to see their audience and make good eye contact because of an outdated practice of turning off the lights. This is one tradition that needs to be retired.

Whether it's lighting, sound, seating arrangement, or the room temperature, set your stage for success. You may get a reputation for being fussier than other presenters, but the results will be worth it.

2
Slide Preparation

I need to say a few words about this section.

Because the majority of modern presentations revolve around PowerPoint slides, everybody wants to know how to better use this software and design more attractive and compelling slides.

These topics demand an in-depth treatment. They don't lend themselves to the kind of tips-for-improvement format this book is built around. Therefore, I'm not going to wade into them. Instead, I would recommend that you go through one of the many good books about PowerPoint and slide design. One that I found useful was *Teach Yourself Visually: Power-Point 2003* by Nancy Muir. PowerPoint 2007 versions by other authors are currently available on Amazon.com.

My contribution to your slide work is the following seven tips that will lead to immediate improvement in your presentations, even if you barely understand PowerPoint and graphic design is something you happily leave to others.

Craft Your Message First, Then Your Slides

Computers have made creating slide presentations easy. Professional quality slides are just mouse clicks away.

Turn on the computer. Open up your favorite presentation software. Start producing slides.

This would be nothing but good news except that it has led to the loss of something critical to a good presentation: a cohesive narrative...a story. Presentations have become fragmented collections of bullet points and graphics.

How does this happen?

It is the result of presenters going straight to slide production when it's time to plan a presentation. In fact, creating slides has become synonymous with planning a presentation.

What's wrong with that? Well, consider what happens when you take this approach. Inevitably, you start building a collection of bullet points. *I better make this point. And that should be mentioned. Also, I can't forget to include this.* The bullet points, with graphs and charts interspersed, pile up. If you have a few relevant slides from other presentations, they also go into the mix.

The result is a presentation that is made up of many separately planned pieces of information. And, because it was built piece by piece, it gets delivered piece by piece. Individual slides may have their own message, but the overall presentation lacks a narrative flow the audience can easily follow.

Audience members need a narrative, a story. If they can

follow along as one point leads to the next, they are much
more likely to understand and recall what they hear.

Think of the last time you said to someone, in a conversation, "I'm not following what you're saying." What did the
other person do? He or she probably paused, took a breath,
and said something like: "Okay, let me go through it step-
by-step." Then they did their best to "walk you through it"
from one point to the next. Notice the language: *step-by-
step, walk you through it.*

Presenters used to do a better job of "walking" their audiences through a message. The slide-making realities they
faced motivated them to first work out the story they wanted
to tell.

Before personal computers, creating a professional-looking
slide show meant having 35mm slides made. This took time
and money. I can remember waiting days for the slides to
be done. Then, when the bill came in, it was computed on
dollars per slide.

Given what was involved, it made sense to *first* work out
what you wanted to say, *then* work out what slides would
be needed. By having first worked out your message—your
"story"—you avoided expensive, time-consuming changes
to the slide deck.

When this approach was taken, the slides were a boiled-down
representation of your story. Consequently, your story naturally reemerged as you went through the slides.

With today's make-the-slides-first approach, a narrative is
much less likely to reemerge when a presentation is given.

47

After all, how is something going to reemerge if it was not there to begin with?

Revelation in a Restaurant

Several years ago I was asked to follow up a presentation skills workshop with an evening coaching session. The session was for two consultants who were a week away from presenting at a convention. They were having trouble putting the presentation together and their managers were becoming concerned.

Their concern was justified. These two gentlemen were struggling with their message.

They *had* created dozens of slides. They *had not* worked out what they wanted to say.

I asked them to take me through the presentation, and within minutes they were passionately debating slide placement. *It's not working to talk about that first. We should put that slide later. No, I don't think so. If we do that they'll get confused. We should put this one before that one.*

Since they had not worked out their story in advance, they were now engaged in what I call Slide Show Scrabble. The object of the game: Get the slides arranged so they spell out some kind of message.

Even highly accomplished Slide Show Scrabble players rarely succeed. They typically settle for stringing together mini-narratives. *First we can use the research slides to talk about the market conditions. Then we can show them the strategy slides and talk about that. Probably the best thing to do after that is move into the budget stuff.*

Chapter 2 Slide Preparation

These guys needed to close up their laptops and work out their message, without worrying about the slides. But, they didn't want to do that. They felt that that would be going backward. They had a full set of slides and they needed to stay focused on how to organize them.

In order to get them away from their slides I had to declare a food break. We went to a nearby restaurant and ordered sandwiches. While we waited for our food, I conducted an experiment. I asked them to tell me more about the special project featured in their presentation. Without hesitation they launched into a fluid overview of their work and its promising results. Full of enthusiasm, they took turns, playing off of each other in a dynamic—impromptu—team "presentation."

When the food arrived, I asked if they realized what had just happened. To their credit, they immediately understood. Free from the tyranny of slides, they had smoothly run through the message they wanted to tell. They had told me the story their convention audience needed to hear.

When our meal was done, we went back to the office and let their "restaurant story" guide our work for the rest of the evening. We edited old slides, created new slides, and put together a presentation that flowed beautifully. They learned how quickly the slides come together when the story has been worked out.

For an immediate, substantial improvement in your presentations, put message planning *before* slide production. Your messages will be smoother, easier to follow, and more memorable.

A Recall Bonus

Let me mention a bonus speakers get from creating strong narratives.

Every speaker is concerned about remembering content. *Will I be able to stay on track? What if I forget what to say?*

Pick up any book on memory techniques and it will instruct you to create links between the items you want to remember. In a presentation, these links are called transitions. *Now that we have gone over the ordering process, let's look at how the warehouse assembles the shipment.*

If your presentation tells a story, transitions come naturally. You know what to say next because it flows from your current point.

Think of the last time you were at a dinner party telling a story. Remember how your friends interrupted you constantly to editorialize and make fun? Did they throw you off track? Not likely. You kept getting right back on your story. You just knew what was next.

In contrast, imagine if you had been trying to recite a list of things. A couple of interruptions and you would have thrown up your hands: "Oh great, now you made me lose my place!" Without a story line to follow, you easily forget what to say next.

A presentation without a story is, essentially, a list of points—a memory problem waiting to happen.

In the future be the very rare presenter who plans the message first and then creates slides.

Chapter 2 Slide Preparation

Make Your Visuals for the Audience

An audience-centered presentation should feature slides created for the benefit of the audience. That's a rather obvious principle, don't you think?

Well, it may be obvious, but its application is rare. Presenters routinely assign the lowest priority to their live audience when preparing slides.

Their first priority is themselves. They create slides to be their notes. In an earlier era they may have referred to written notes, but now they want the slides to tell them what to say next. This is what they are admitting to when they confess that their slides are a crutch. *I need my slides!* What goes up on the screen is what will best spur their thinking, not what will best spur the audience's thinking.

Slides that are speaker notes can be either anemic or crammed with too much content. Some presenters just need reminder notes, so they create slides with cryptic phrases that mean nothing to the audience. Others need the slide show equivalent of a script, so their bullet points are complete paragraphs in ten-point type. Either way, the slides are frustrating to an audience.

Further pushing the live audience down the priority list is concern about people who will *not* be at the presentation. This group includes managers who want to preview the presentation and others who have scheduling conflicts. For these people, presenters create slides that can be turned into a printed handout. They want to distribute something that is detailed enough to make attendance at the live presentation unnecessary. This priority favors the full-paragraph, script slides.

The next time you put together a set of slides, be more audience centered than the typical presenter. Think about what the people sitting in front of you will benefit from most. What do they need to easily follow along and understand your message? What will most enlighten them?

If you need a handout, realize that a good slide show is not a good handout—and a good handout is not a good slide show. If you don't want to go to the trouble of creating a separate document, consider using the Speaker Notes option in PowerPoint. This option was originally created so that speakers could print their notes below their slides. You can use the same capability to print up all the detail a reader would need. Using this approach you're not tempted to cram all the detail onto the slides. The live audience gets easy-to-read slides, and the handout crowd gets all the detail they would have heard had they been there.

When your live audience is best served by your slides, your priorities are right.

Plan to Go Without a Slide

If your presentation is a continuous slide show, what can fail to develop?

The answer: a personal connection with the audience members. Their attention is fixed on the screen instead of on you.

Some presenters like it that way. *I don't want them paying attention to me! It makes me nervous!* These presenters prefer to be a voice off to the side or in the back of the room. Even better is to have the lights off and become a disembodied voice in a dark room.

Other presenters worry about losing their place or going off on a tangent if they don't always have a slide showing.

Showing slides without a break is standard operating procedure in corporate America. If a presentation is formal enough to require slides, then it is *all* slides *all* the time.

As radical as it sounds, you don't *have* to have a slide showing at all times. In fact, your presentations would immediately become stronger if you didn't. A blank screen redirects the audience's attention back to you. Consider what you could do with this full, undivided attention.

Picture this. You are presenting a detailed budget analysis. There is evidence of chronic overspending in one area. Past warnings about this situation have gone unheeded. Your message that "something must be done" needs to get through and register with these decision makers.

After pointing out the offending numbers, you turn off your slides and walk to the center of the room. As you do this, you express your desire to say a few things about the situation in this budget category. Then, close to the audience, eye to eye, you talk to your listeners instead of to another slide. You elaborate on your concerns and, potentially, field questions. Only after you have made your point do you walk back to the side of the screen and resume your slide show.

Did you get attention? Has your concern registered? You better believe it. And, you enhanced your image as a strong communicator who actively engages audiences.

Also, you have increased the persuasive potential of your message. People "buy"—products, services, ideas, proposals, priorities—from people. Enhancing your personal connection with the audience has helped you more effectively "sell" your message.

Often in workshops I will stop a presenter and have him or her repeat something using this approach. Usually it is something easily remembered without a slide, such as an anecdote. Afterward I will ask the presenter and the other workshop participants—the audience—what they thought about that part of the presentation. They respond the same way every time. The speaker talks about being a bit uncomfortable without a slide, but the audience praises the results. *It just looked strong. She came across more confident.*

Okay, you say. It's worth a try. But what about the mechanics of stopping and restarting a slide show?

Fortunately, we are well past the days of putting cardboard in front of the projector lens or covering up an overhead transparency with paper.

If, as most people, you are using PowerPoint, you just have to press the letter "B" on your computer's keyboard. The screen will go blank, and stay that way, until you press "B" again to revive your slide. With some laptops you can conveniently revive your show with the next slide by pressing the space bar.

Some projection units come with a remote control unit that has a "blank screen" button. This can be used in place of the "B" key if—and this is a big if—the button actually works. It's amazing how few of them do.

My advice is to buy your own remote control. Get one of the models that works through the USB port on your laptop and has a "blank screen" button. Then, if the projection unit's remote is missing or not working, you're still in business.

Be Courageous

If you start using this blank-screen technique you will immediately stand out from your peers. I guarantee it. It is *so* rare to find a speaker who will do it. Even people who know how it's done, like the idea, appreciate its effectiveness, and have witnessed its impact, will not do it. This is one presentation technique that is in no danger of being overused—despite its strong potential.

When I ask workshop participants for an example of something they are glad they learned, the most frequently given answer is "the B key." *I can't wait to give it a try!*

Fast forward to the next time I see them and they are "still looking for an opportunity to work it in." As soon as they left the workshop, the all-slides-all-the-time corporate culture reasserted itself.

Not long ago, I had the pleasure of working with a corporate vice president who was an exception to the norm. For his company's annual leadership conference he and I came up with a message that only incorporated a handful of slides. A good part of the time he would be stage-center, sans slide.

He was nervous about it. *The CEO is a slide freak who wants to see everybody's slides before the conference.* But he stuck with the plan, and the feedback afterward was excellent. He was particularly proud of one e-mail from a fellow executive who commented on the poise and leadership he exhibited.

Many factors went into this vice president's success. It was not just about going without slides. However, he proved that the "B" key can be used for strong effect without causing a scandal, even with a CEO who is a "slide freak."

Try it out. Experiment. The first couple of times you may just want to blank the screen when a discussion breaks out or someone asks a question. Later you can go the next step and purposely plan slide breaks when you want your audience's undivided attention. A safe time to try it is when you are telling a story and do not need a slide to augment your memory.

I personally make it a point to always start and end my presentations without a slide. If I have a title slide, I only show it while the audience is getting settled. Then I blank the screen and concentrate on establishing a personal connection. Undistracted, eye-to-eye contact is equally as important at the end, particularly when asking for an audience response.

Remember, you want to be a powerful communicator, not slide show narrator!

Be Visual With Visuals

As I mentioned in an earlier segment, a dirty little secret about presentation slides is that they are made more for the speaker than for the audience. They are blown-up, projected-on-a-screen speaker notes.

And, because they are speaker notes, they look like speaker notes.

reading from slides

In the worst case, they are fully written-out scripts. Slide after slide consists of full paragraphs and long sentences arbitrarily divided by bullet points. Instead of staring down at a printed script, the speaker stares at the screen and reads. Audience members look to the doors for possible escape.

More common are slides with bulleted phrases. Fortunately, speakers are less likely to read them word for word; but, they are still all words.

Visuals are more effective when they are truly visual. By this I mean they feature graphics, pictures, and—sometimes—videos.

What's the old saying? A picture equals a thousand words. It's still true.

I once had a gentleman in a workshop who practiced presenting a request for more employees. The thrust of his argument was that the six employees he had were not enough for the one hundred job assignments they were expected to complete each month. I expected him to describe this situation with a bullet-point slide, but instead he showed a slide filled with one hundred file folder icons and six stick people down in the lower left-hand corner. Even though it was simple and roughly designed, the visual impact easily exceeded anything bullet points could have accomplished. At once you were struck by the immensity of one hundred jobs being handled by only six people.

Before you settle for bullet points, go the extra mile and see if you can come up with a way to visually make your point. In our media-driven, visual culture, the need to move beyond just words is more necessary than ever.

Navigate the Slide Deck Smoothly

A dynamic, interactive presentation does not always follow the slide order you intended. A question might send you back to a previously shown slide. A senior manager might demand that you jump ahead.

Typically, presenters accomplish these jumps by quickly running through the intervening slides until they reach the one they need. Or, they switch to a view of all their slides and search with their mouse for the one they want. There is an easier, more professional way to move around in your slide deck.

When using PowerPoint, you can jump directly to any slide in your presentation by simply typing that slide's number and hitting the "Enter" key. Then, when it's time to return to the slide you originally were on, you enter its number and again tap "Enter." Quick. Easy. No fumbling around.

Of course, it will help if you have a numbered list of your slides sitting next to your laptop. You can type them up or let PowerPoint list them for you. The PowerPoint list comes from collapsing the outline of your presentation to titles only and then hitting the "Print" command.

Smoothly navigating your slide deck out of order adds an impressive fluidness to discussion management.

Don't Fall Victim to the Technology

Visual design guru Edward Tufte warns against creating slides that showcase technology more than the information they are supposed to be communicating. This can happen when a presenter gets carried away with elaborate design and animation. Tufte says you have reached this point when the audience stops commenting on the data and starts saying things like "Boy, isn't it amazing what they can do with computers."

Tufte is warning against letting technology take over and do too much. To that I would add a warning about those times when technology goes on strike and refuses to do anything.

We have all witnessed it: otherwise confident presenters brought to their knees by computers and projectors that refuse to cooperate. *I can't believe this! It was working perfectly a minute ago!* They test the wires and push the magic keys, and still a blank screen defiantly stares back at them.

When this happens to you—and it will; nobody escapes— keep yourself focused on your primary mission. You have a message to communicate. You also have a need to communicate it in a way that positions you as a confident communicator. You should not let the technology undermine either one of those priorities.

What does it look like when technology is undermining a presenter? A huddle forms around the computer or projection unit. As the rest of the audience becomes restless, the presenter and earnest helpers from the audience take turns pushing buttons, tapping keys, and jiggling wires. Multiple cures are suggested. *Maybe you should turn it off and then back on.* Eventually a call goes out to the technical support group: "Send the cavalry!" Then, while the tech guy is being paged, the boss steps in with: "Maybe we should move on to something else and come back to John's presentation later."

Not good.

Do not let this happen to you. Have your alternatives planned in advance. Protection against laptop problems includes putting your presentation on a memory stick for possible transfer to another laptop. Also, have hard copies of your slides on hand.

Then, give yourself a two-minute rule. If the equipment refuses to work after two minutes, hit the "Off" button and start delivering your message as best as you can without the slides. If you have hard copies for everybody, this should not be difficult. But even if you don't, start talking.

Your presentation may not be as smooth as it otherwise would have been. It may also run shorter than you intended. However, you will have avoided the more serious problem of losing your audience.

Don't keep fussing with the equipment. If it isn't working, it isn't working. Move on. Be decisive. And, whatever you do, do not keep making references to the equipment problems. *Of course, I could have shown you this information in graph form if only my computer had not decided to act up.* Let it go. It is not in your best interest to keep reminding the audience members what they are not getting.

You are charged with delivering a message, not with delivering a slide show.

Take Ownership of Corporate Slide Presentations

Before leaving this section on slides, I need to say something about presenting with a slide deck your company has prepared for you.

Chapter 2 Slide Preparation

Far from making things easier, your company has actually handed you one of the biggest challenges a presenter can face.

When you create your own presentation, it reflects your thinking. This is true even if you make slides before you work out your story. At least the individual slides and their sequencing follow a logic that makes sense to you. A packaged presentation, on the other hand, reflects someone else's thinking. Or, to be more accurate, it reflects *several* other people's thinking. It's a patchwork of priorities that may appear cohesive only because the graphics department gave the slides a consistent look.

If you have worked with one of these babies before you know what it's like. In your preliminary review you keep running into slide sequences that don't make sense—at least not to you. *Why does this slide follow that one? It would make more sense to finish the market analysis before introducing strategy options. I don't get it.*

Rehearsals can be frustrating affairs that never get you past the point of feeling like you're trying to sit in a car seat adjusted for somebody else. Some portions are smooth; others are not. In the end, you make it work even if it is "a bit choppy in places."

Before you resign yourself to a presentation that falls short of something you personally authored, consider a few steps that will help you take fuller ownership of it.

First, analyze the presentation's flow by trying to work out how you would transition to each slide. In other words, think through how you might talk your way from one slide to the next. *The negative crime trend you see here is broken down by crime type on this next slide.*

As you do this, a narrative (i.e., story) that makes sense to you will begin to take shape. Also, you will identify where this narrative breaks down despite your best efforts. You know you have hit one of these breakdown points when you can't think of anything to say that will get you smoothly to the next slide.

Before you forget them, jot down your transitions on photocopies of the slides. Then turn your attention to the breakdown points. Talk to the slide deck authors. What did they have in mind for these points in the presentation? If they can't help, experiment with different slide sequences (if you are allowed to do such a thing). If and when rearranging the slide order doesn't help, consider dropping a slide or two—again, if you have permission to do so. Typically, an awkward slide is the brainchild of a management reviewer. *Make sure you include a slide with some of the most frequent comments we heard in the focus groups. I don't care where you put it; just make sure it's in there somewhere.* And with that you have a slide that fits in like a patch on a new suit.

When all else fails, camouflage narrative breaks by making them seem deliberate. You can do this by soliciting audience participation. *Before I continue further (blank out the screen) I'd like to hear what kind of customer feedback you've been getting.* Or, if you don't want to get the audience involved, you can take a couple minutes for an anecdotal break. *This trend toward less customer loyalty became real to me in a series of meetings I recently had. One in particular stands out. I was meeting with…*

Once you have worked out your slide-to-slide narrative flow, it's time to turn your attention to the individual slides. As much as possible you want to flow within the slides, not just between them. The graphic slides should be the easiest to deal with because they have the least amount of preordained wording. Bullet point slides take more work.

Work out as many transitions between bullet points as you can. The more you transition from point to point, the smoother your delivery becomes. Realistically you're not going to be able to transition between all points because the presentation authors randomly grouped so many of them. Do what you can; every bit helps.

Once you have your narrative flow worked out, it's time to go to the final step and add some personal touches. Anywhere you can add a personal story, example, analogy, or some audience interaction, this company presentation is going to become more *your* presentation.

If a bullet point says, "Ensure regular partnering between sales and marketing," bring that concept alive with an example of what such partnering actually looks like. If you can draw this example from your own experience, all the better.

If a slide describes action items that are potentially controversial, plan to take a few minutes for thoughts from the audience. With a chance to participate, audience members will often start taking some ownership of the message. When a message goes from being the *company's*, to being *yours*, to being *ours*, success is within reach.

So, in the future, when you get handed a completed slide deck, despair not. You can make it yours by hammering out a narrative one transition at a time, and by injecting your own color.

3
Practice

Practice Changes in Everyday Life

Participants in presentation skills workshops like to compare the experience with taking a golf lesson. When they first try something new, their overall performance goes down instead of up. It's frustrating, but it's the natural result of concentrating hard on overriding an old habit with something new and unfamiliar. If they stick at it and turn the new behavior into a habit, they will perform better than ever.

Unfortunately, many people don't stick to it. They go back to their old ways because they don't want to risk a performance problem in any presentation they do. Their mistake is in thinking that skill practice is only possible in actual presentations.

You can—and should—practice skill changes in everyday life. Then you can establish new habits without taking risks in front of important presentation audiences.

If, for example, you need better eye contact when you present, you have dozens of interactions every day in which you can practice. You have one-on-one conversations everywhere you go. You speak at meetings. You talk to multiple people at meals. In each and every instance you can include some practice at having better eye contact.

I had a gentleman in training who tried eye contact practice in one of the workshop breaks. He went down to the Starbucks in the lobby and made it a point to look the counter person in the eye when he placed his order. It was hard because he is a shy person, but he declared it a small triumph and committed to regular practice wherever he goes.

Maybe eye contact is not the new habit you need. Maybe you need to eliminate the use of a word or phrase. If so, every conversation is a potential practice opportunity. If you need to speak more slowly or pause more often, every ring of the phone signals a possible practice session.

Of course there are a few presentation skills you don't use in your daily encounters. For example, you don't show slides everywhere you go. You don't use PowerPoint when you speak at the dinner table (hopefully). This kind of practice is going to have to be planned and scheduled. However, most of the behaviors involved in presenting are part of daily interactions.

Practice in your day-to-day encounters, and the new habits you want will form. Then, when you go to the front of the room to present, they will be there without you thinking about it.

Chapter 3 Practice

Practice—Out Loud

In our own minds we are all eloquent.

As we think through a presentation, one thought follows another with reassuring smoothness.

Then we stand in front of the audience and open our mouth. Out comes a message that is—how can we say this nicely?— "rough in a few spots."

The problem lies in how our mind conspires with itself. During silent, mental practice, it conveniently skips over spots in the message that are not fully worked out. We trust the words will come when we need them.

Sometimes they do. Often they don't.

If I was coaching someone who was willing to make only one change to how they prepare for presentations, I would urge them to start practicing **out loud**. Trying to verbalize a message is the surest way to expose—while there is still time to make changes—the parts that are rough.

I like the way Peggy Noonan puts it in her book *On Speaking Well*. She advises that you practice out loud and then "Where you falter, alter."

I joke sometimes that my dogs have had to listen to all my presentations. Through droopy eyelids they watch me pace back and forth, explaining my slides and making my case to the walls. While I ignore their obvious disinterest, I determine if I can really say what I intend to say. Inevitably I falter and have to alter.

Once, while I was teaching at a large corporation, a class participant pointed to the company's CEO as an example of a natural speaker. *You can just tell he's a born speaker.* Immediately, one of her associates disagreed. This second person explained that her office was right next door to the CEO's practice room. *By the time you hear him speak, I've heard his talk so many times I could give it.* She explained that he routinely spent time in this conference room, pacing around the table, practicing out loud what he would say and how he would say it.

But I don't want to sound rehearsed.

Have you ever used that excuse for not practicing? You don't want to practice, so you rationalize that it's actually good that you are not practicing. If you practiced, after all, you would get that unappealing rehearsed sound.

Good, effective practice does not lead to a rehearsed sound. The key is to remain flexible in your word usage and not practice a word-for-word recitation. Let yourself say things differently with each practice run. The point is not to memorize a script but to identify rough segments and smooth them out.

Resist the temptation to only practice those parts you think need work. This may seem like a responsible shortcut. It's not. Until you have actually tried to say something, you can't be sure it will flow well. Practice all the way through.

Be forewarned. The first few minutes of out-loud practice will always feel awkward. After all, most of us don't like the sound of our own voices and we're not in the habit of talking to ourselves. The discomfort will inevitably pass as you get engrossed in the message.

Practice Your Introduction the Most

Although I have met a few presenters who start out calm and become nervous as their presentation progresses, they are rare. Most people experience their highest level of anxiety at the beginning of their talk. After speaking for a few minutes they settle down. I can't tell you how many times someone has said to me, "Once I get started, I'm okay."

While it is reassuring to know that calmness will soon come, what happens in that first one or two minutes can make a poor first impression. This is particularly the case if your nervousness causes memory loss. *My mind goes blank. I can't remember what I was going to say.* It doesn't serve you well to start off babbling, even if you get on track quickly.

If you know from experience that you start out nervous, put extra practice into your introduction. You want to get to the point that you can do it on automatic pilot. After you have practiced the whole presentation a few times, keep practicing your introduction whenever you get a chance.

Then, when you first step to the front of the room, you have the mental equivalent of a firm handrail to hold onto. You can start strong even if the early jitters are making it hard to concentrate on what you need to say.

Practice your introduction the most. It will set you up for early confidence.

Get Help Toughening Up

When a big piece of business is riding on a presentation, it is not unusual for managers to sit in on a rehearsal. Typically, they act as coaches, offering suggested changes and making predictions about the real audience. *You've got to include a slide about our technical support program. We've worked with these people before and they want to know that problems are going to be solved fast.*

One client company I have worked with over the years takes this practice to a higher level of difficulty than most. Senior executives fill the room for a final, full-scale dress rehearsal. During this rehearsal, they play the role of a real audience. They interrupt regularly, ask penetrating questions, and generally give the presenters a tough time. They stay in character and don't give advice until the presentation is over and it is time for a debriefing.

The first time I sat through one of these rehearsals, I was amazed by the intensity of it. In fact, I worried about the presenters. I was concerned that their confidence was getting damaged. What good were they going to be wounded and unsure of themselves?

As it turned out, they were okay because they were not surprised by the intensity. These grueling rehearsals were part of the corporate culture. Because they expected to be drilled—and potentially made to stumble a bit—their morale and confidence remained high. It also helped that the senior people made it a point to stick around afterward and give them plenty of encouragement.

What impressed me was the benefit the presenters derived from this rehearsal. They displayed extraordinary poise in front of the real customer audience. Afterward, I asked them about it and they said the real presentation was "nothing" compared to the senior-management rehearsal. They had been toughened up like athletes who practice while wearing heavy weights.

Your organization may not have a practice of setting up dress rehearsals with senior managers; few do. However, with the help of your close associates, you can get some toughening up before a big performance. The key is to have them play the role of a demanding audience *before* they play the role of advisor. You need actual practice dealing with serious challenges to your message. Then, when you get in front of the real audience, it will not be a shock. In fact, like the team I told you about, it may seem easier.

Also, don't just use this technique for presentations to outside audiences. It is an excellent idea for getting ready for internal presentations to senior management. I have noticed that people are very good at putting themselves into senior roles. Sometimes, they will actually take on the speaking mannerisms of specific executives.

Rather than get anxious about the possible challenges you may face in an upcoming presentation, make them happen in a realistic rehearsal. Then when you face the real audience it will be a case of "been there, done that."

4
Working
With A Team

Draft the Best Team

Years ago I was getting a team ready for a big presentation. A sizeable piece of new business was at stake, so the client company was pulling out all the stops. For two full weeks I practically lived with the presenters. I even flew with them to the potential customer's headquarters and holed up in a hotel for a final round of rehearsals.

My mandate was simple: get this team to the point where it could win that contract despite exceptionally strong competition.

Early on it became clear to me that one of the team members was not going to improve enough in time for the main event. He was a weak link with decades of bad habits and little inclination to change. Unfortunately, he was the senior team member and slated to oversee the new business if it was successfully won! You could say the situation was "politically touchy."

With a mandate to win, I felt compelled to go to my main contact at the company and express my concerns. The next thing I knew I was shut up in a room with the company president, who had only been told I had something to tell him. Nobody in the company wanted to leave fingerprints on this situation.

I spoke my piece and the team leader had his role in the presentation dramatically reduced. To his credit he graciously accepted the change and continued to work hard on refining the proposal.

The team went on to win the contract, even though it was learned later that one of the competitors—the incumbent— had been assured of the business. Taking the lead manager off the presentation team was not *the* deciding factor, but it was definitely an important factor in the win.

Just as with sports teams, successful presentation teams depend on a strong player selection. The more skill, talent, and experience you take into a presentation, the higher the performance potential you have. This potential is particularly critical in fast-paced corporate environments where limited time is available for preparation and rehearsal.

This is not a controversial concept, but its application is controversial. The makeup of a presentation team is often driven by office or departmental politics. Even when the politics can be navigated, there is a playground sense of fairness that calls for everybody to get a chance to play and show their stuff. And, finally, there is my favorite: "He has to be the lead presenter, he's the boss!"

Be smart about the politics.

Give people a chance to gain experience whenever possible.

Don't make the boss prove who has more power.

But *do* look for every opportunity to assemble high-potential teams. In the long run success creates more opportunities for everyone.

Plan Together

The last time I had my car inspected there was a big banner on the inspection station wall that said "**T**ogether **E**mployees **A**ccomplish **M**ore: **TEAM.**" Teamwork has become such a popular concept that even the guys who check our car exhaust are expected to team together for success.

This teams-are-better philosophy is behind many presentations. But often the "team" in "team presentation" is on the surface only. In reality, three or four solo artists prepare individual messages and then appear together on the day of the presentation. Their planning teamwork was limited to working out how they would divide up the overall topic.

Even if contradictions and inconsistencies are caught and repaired in a rehearsal, the presentation is not going to be as good as it could have been.

Plan your team presentation as a team. Together, work out the overall flow and then make sure everybody knows what everybody else is developing. Touch base regularly as content ideas develop.

With close coordination each part can complement the other parts. Ideas can build across segments. References to the other segments can be planned, built in, and rehearsed. The end result is a more integrated team presentation than people are accustomed to hearing.

Plan the In-Between Parts

The best team presentations come across as a single, unbroken message. The best teams speak with one voice. That is why I emphasize planning together.

You might say: "We do plan together! We work closely through the whole process."

Excellent! But I suspect there may still be some places in your team presentation that you and your associates have not consistently coordinated. I call them the "in-between parts." Specifically, I'm talking about the handoffs from one speaker to the next.

If you have ever watched a relay race at a track and field event, you know how important the handoffs are. If a runner fumbles handing the baton to the next runner, the team loses its rhythm and momentum.

A poor handoff in a team presentation causes a similar loss of rhythm and momentum. Instead of a smooth transition from one portion of the narrative to the next, the audience experiences a clunky break in the flow. *So, that's pretty much all I had to say about the market research. Now, aahh, I believe we planned to have John talk about strategy. So, aahh, John, why don't you pick it up?*

Then, the presentation becomes suspended in air while the speakers change places in an awkward dance. The next presenter shuffles about getting comfortable and checking to see how the remote control works. Finally, with an equal lack of eloquence, this presenter makes some unplanned, useless comments about the previous segment. *So, I hope you found that interesting about the research. I know I did when I first heard it. It's amazing what studies can reveal.*

Imagine the same kind of message break in the middle of an individual's presentation. Your first thought would be that something is wrong. The speaker has had a brain lapse or the projector is acting up. Whatever it is, the flow of the message has been broken.

When I'm asked to coach a presentation team, I will typically ask to hear the whole presentation in its preliminary form. I need to assess what has been done and determine what needs the most attention. Inevitably, as each speaker finishes he or she will say something like: "With that, I turn it over to Harry/Mary/Larry." I'll then ask what the "turn it over" sounds like. Maybe one in a hundred presenters can tell me what they are going to say. It's just assumed that some impromptu comments will be sufficient. *You know. Blah blah blah. Blah blah blah. Whatever.*

As I push to learn what the "blah, blah, blah" is going to

consist of, clients will act surprised. *You really want us to work out what we are going to say.* Yes, I do.

Just as a single presenter needs to smoothly transition from one part of a presentation to the next, multiple speakers on a team need to transition smoothly from one speaker to the next. It's essential if the presentation is going to come across as a single, well-coordinated message.

Each presenter should summarize what he or she has covered and then link it to what the next speaker is going to cover. *So as you can see, both divisions have planned their part of the project so as to make efficient use of common resources. Now, I would like to turn it over to Bob, who will detail these savings along with the proposed budget.*

With a good transition it's not necessary for the next presenter to begin with a reference to the previous speaker. Enough has been said. However, the next presenter can reference back if it's not redundant. A good clue that something is going to be redundant is that it begins with "As my associate just said." Usually it's better to start right out with an attention getter for the new segment.

In addition to working out the transitional wording, thought must be given to how the slide show will be handled. It's not going to look professional if the previous speaker's last slide lingers on the screen while the next speaker gets positioned. One option is for the departing speaker to put up a highlighted agenda slide or a title slide for the next section as part of the transition. Another option is for the departing speaker to blank out the screen. The latter approach is advisable if the new speaker is going to have to walk in front of the projector in order to get positioned.

Some teams will attempt to minimize the break between speakers by having the next speaker get positioned while the current speaker fields questions. Usually this involves the current speaker moving to the center of the room while the next speaker gets situated at the lectern. While it sounds good in theory, it rarely works well. Often the next speaker becomes a distraction: first by shuffling around papers and testing the remote control; then by standing there and giving the impression that the previous speaker's question period is holding things up.

It's possible to minimize the break between speakers with just a small amount of logistical planning before the presentation. Make sure all the speakers are seated close to where they will be speaking from and then make sure there is a clear path for changing positions. Familiarize everyone with the equipment and have all notes and materials sorted out and easily accessed. It's a bit like stage planning for a Broadway play. *Exit stage right. New speaker enters stage left.*

Remember, the objective is a team presentation that is so seamless and smooth the audience experiences it as a single presentation.

Plan the Q & A

If you go to a conference and attend a panel discussion, you will typically see a lot of fumbling around as the panel members try to work out who will answer each question. They exchange glances with one another, trying to see if anyone is going to take the initiative and volunteer. If no one does, a negotiation ensues. *Sam, that sounds like something you might want to handle. Well, I've got some thoughts, but it might be better if Susan addresses it from the viewpoint of a specialist.* Eventually, someone answers and the process repeats itself with the next question. It's annoying to sit through, but audience members typically accept the lack of coordination. They understand that these people were thrown together by the conference planner.

Teams do not enjoy the same understanding. When they fumble around handling a question it reflects badly on the whole team. Audience members expect *both* the presentation *and* the Q & A period to be well coordinated. There should be no hesitation, no debating, and no talking over one another.

The two main options for coordinating a team's response to questions are: 1) team leader control, or 2) assigned topics.

If the team leader is going to control things, then he or she takes each question, answers it, or directs it to another team member. It is up to the leader to decide who is going to answer. This person acts as a facilitator and the single point of focus for audience members who have a question.

With the assigned-topic option, it gets worked out in advance who on the team will handle which question categories. *Jim, if there are any questions on pricing, they're yours. Judy, you should jump in if they ask about distribution issues.*

Even with the assigned-topic approach, some leadership control may be needed. Obviously, not all questions will fall nice and neatly into predetermined categories. At the slightest hint of hesitation, the leader needs to jump in and determine whose area a question best falls into.

Whichever approach is decided on, it will need to be explained to the audience at the start of the Q & A period.

One other thing to think about is whether or not the team member answering a question is going to stand up. If the team is in front of a large audience, standing is typically a good idea. If everyone is seated around a conference table it makes more sense to stay seated unless the answering team member has one of the seats along the wall. Then it may be better to stand up.

There are multiple variations of the two approaches I've described. The important thing is not so much *how* you coordinate the Q & A, but that you, in fact, somehow coordinate it. Include this often-neglected issue in your planning and practice sessions.

5
Delivery Strategy

Set the Tone

In the segment on starting strong and ending strong, I talked about the initial impression you make.

It would be misleading to say that the only first impression is the one you make on the audience. In fact, it's a two-way street; the audience will make a first impression on you as well.

You may find yourself in front of a group of openly friendly people who project an eagerness to hear what you have to say. They each shook your hand as they walked into the room; said how much they were looking forward to your talk; and entered right into casual banter with both you and their fellow audience members. The atmosphere is good. You feel encouraged. Success is in the air.

Unfortunately, not every audience is like this. Even when there is no impending confrontation or brewing discontent, the initial "vibes" an audience gives off can be less than encouraging.

Sometimes people walk into the room without acknowledging your presence. Or, if they do make eye contact, their greeting is little more than a mumble. No smiles. No laughter. No friendly chitchat. You find yourself looking around at unreadable expressions in a room that is oddly quiet. *Oh boy.*

It's at times like these that your sensitivity to audiences— normally a very good thing—will start working against you. The atmosphere will begin to pull you down. It will feel like energy is being sucked out of you.

You are experiencing what is known as "emotional contagion." In their book of the same name, E. Hatfield, J. Cacioppo, and R. Rapson describe research that has documented the strong tendency of people to "catch" the emotions of whomever they are associating with.

As a presenter it is imperative that you immediately recognize what is happening and determine not to give into it. If there is going to be any emotional contagion, it is going to be your positive emotions spreading to the audience. In other words, *you* are going to set the tone; not them.

This is not easy. In fact, it is one of the most difficult challenges a speaker can face. But you have to be determined— even if it takes awhile for the audience to start responding positively. Set the tone that you believe is appropriate, be patient, and stay with it.

I say "be patient" because I don't want you overcompensating for a negative or down atmosphere. Some speakers try too hard to quickly change things. They get loud. They chide the audience. They resort to lame humor and laugh too hard. *Good morning, everybody!! Oh, come on now, you can do better than that. Goooood morning! Boy, we're going to have to start making strong coffee and glazed donuts mandatory for all meetings. Hah! Hah!*

Come on too strong and you are liable to get the opposite of what you want. Audience members, who were initially just distracted and tired, now get turned off and actively resist the positive atmosphere you are trying to create.

Establish a reasonable, upbeat tone, and stick with it. Most audiences will come around.

Emotional contagion is a powerful force. Make it work for you instead of becoming its victim.

Remember and Use Names

Did you know that everybody has the same favorite sound? Do you know what it is?

No, it's not the sound of their child's voice, although that's high on the list. Their number one favorite sound is the sound of their own name. Dale Carnegie made this observation in his classic book *How to Win Friends and Influence People*. He strongly recommended that anyone desiring to connect well with people learn names and use them in conversation.

Because a good presentation has a conversational quality to it, Carnegie's advice fits right in. You can connect faster and better with your audience members by taking the trouble to learn their names and use them in your message. Those who hear their name love the sound, and everyone senses a greater familiarity in the room. Also, you score points for your name-learning effort.

I had an experience with this phenomenon when I was distributing materials at a workshop and discovered that someone had forgotten to pack the name tents. I realized I was going to have to work without them, so I made a greater-than-normal effort to learn names. As participants showed up, I introduced myself and concentrated on the name they gave. Also, when no one was paying attention, I would drift back to the head table and scribble the names I'd learned on a rough seating diagram.

From the first minute of the workshop, I started using names. It wasn't long before some whispered conversation led to someone raising a hand and asking how I knew so many people, given that it was my first time at the company. I acted innocently confused by the question and assured them I didn't know anybody prior to the workshop. "But you know everybody's name" was the comeback.

Even though we had exchanged names and shook hands—and there were only ten of them—they had no expectation that I would remember what everybody had said. The fact that I *had* remembered led them to believe that I wasn't the stranger they thought I was. Later on, a couple of them included on their workshop evaluations how impressed they were with my name recall.

This experience, and many more since then, have shown me just how powerful name recall can be for a presenter. It takes some work—particularly when your mind is on your presentation—but it pays off. The fast setup in familiarity with your audience generates early openness to what you are saying. That you paid attention to people's names motivates them to pay attention to you.

Of course I know what you're going to say: "I'm lousy with names." So try my seating chart technique. You only have to remember names long enough to jot them down. Then you can put the chart next to your notes or laptop. It's unlikely anyone will notice that you are regularly refreshing your memory. I've also learned that I can fill in some blanks as I listen to what people are saying during discussions. They will use each other's names from time to time.

You can also study name-recall techniques. I recently dug out my aged copy of Harry Lorayne's book *Remembering People*. Lorayne gained fame years ago on TV by remembering all the names of people in studio audiences. Even though the book's copyright is 1975, used copies are available at Amazon.com. Great stuff!

Plan Your Dive and Dive Your Plan

Scuba divers are a careful lot. They have to be. It's dangerous in the deep blue sea.

They carefully plan a dive. Then, when they're in the water, they stick to the plan. They determine, in advance, to avoid spur-of-the-moment changes that have not been thought through. Their philosophy is simple: Plan your dive. Dive your plan.

Most presenters would benefit from a similar philosophy when they take to the podium. Having planned—and hopefully practiced—what they will say, they should say what they planned.

Presenters chronically deviate from their planned comments. If they were scuba divers, half of them would drown. Metaphorically, many of them do.

They make an unplanned comment that leads to political problems. *I didn't mean it the way it sounded!* They go off on a tangent, taking the focus off their central theme. *Now where was I?* They throw in a story that burns up precious time they can't recover. *Wow! The time got away from me.*

And then there is the biggest gamble of them all: They go for a laugh with something "funny" that just occurred to them. It is amateur night at the comedy club and the audience did not catch the humor. *Oh, boy. This is not good.*

I'm personally familiar with the comedy temptation. I love to make people laugh. When my prepared material is going well and people have big smiles on their faces, I don't want it to end. That's when I'm tempted to adlib. Sometimes it works; other times I sorely wish I had quit while I was ahead.

Think about your last presentation. During the planning process you scratched things out and reworded your thoughts multiple times. You reworked slides, moving around bullet points and modifying graphics. You dropped and added slides, and changed the sequence of others. You practiced out loud, identifying rough spots and polishing them. In the end, a considerable amount of your initial thinking needed to be modified and polished before you were ready to go.

In contrast, changes you make *during* the presentation lack any of this careful consideration. Something you probably would have scratched out and forgotten during the planning process is now coming out of your mouth in raw form.

If you deviate from your planned material it can be like handing in a written report with last-minute Post-it notes slapped on several pages. You would never do that with a written document, so why do it with a presentation?

Trust your planning. Believe in it. What you carefully crafted in advance has the highest probability of success. Changes you make on the fly will have the highest probability of failure.

Plan your presentation. Present your plan.

Be Responsive, Not Reactive

Good presenters know the difference between being responsive to an audience and being reactive.

When you are a responsive speaker, you carry your concern for the audience's needs and wants right into the delivery of your presentation. You stay aware and keep your antennae up. If you detect confusion, you clarify. If resistance shows itself, you work to resolve it. If something you say strikes a responsive chord, you recognize the potential and add emphasis.

It's not unlike being a salesperson with a potential buyer: constantly listening, watching, and tailoring the message to fit the unique "audience" currently sitting across the table.

This is productive responsiveness. The presenter maintains the initiative, staying in control and on-message.

All is well until being responsive slips over the line into being reactive. An audience member who appears bored causes you to speed up and skip over important material. Or, a couple of antagonists cause you to start acting defensive and apologizing for shortcomings in your proposal.

When I think of my own experience slipping from responsive to reactive, I inevitably think of this workshop I conducted years ago. I can look back on it now and laugh, but it was not good. I let my perception of one person significantly affect my performance.

Throughout the whole two days of the workshop, this individual kept falling asleep. I interpreted her behavior as a sign that I was boring. So, I became more animated. When she persisted in nodding off, I ratcheted the energy and animation even higher. By the end of the workshop I was practically dancing on the tables. The other people in the class had to be wondering what in the world was going on. *This guy really needs to cut back on the caffeine.*

After the workshop this woman came up to me and apologized for dozing off. She explained that it had nothing to do with the workshop, but was the result of her going for several nights without sleep because of a colicky child. I politely finished our conversation and then proceeded to collapse from exhaustion.

Even if she *had* been bored, my reactive behavior would have been wrong. I had planned a workshop that targeted the needs of the group, and everyone except her was paying attention. I had also started with a tone and level of animation appropriate for the group. But, when I started to fixate on her, I stopped being responsive to the group and became reactive to an individual.

If you catch yourself starting to react to one or two people, pause. Look around the room. Refocus on the larger audience. Switch back to being responsive to the many instead of reactive to the few.

Leave the Audience Alone

Picture this. You're at a comedy club and the comedian on stage is dying. Hardly anyone is laughing and the room is uncomfortably quiet. What does the comedian do? He or she probably starts commenting on the audience's lack of support. *Boy, this is a tough crowd. I've heard more laughs at a funeral. Is anybody awake?*

What is the comedian hoping to accomplish? Answer: get the audience members to start being more supportive. Will it work? No.

Oh, they might start laughing a bit more. But it won't be a genuine reaction to the funniness of the material. They will make an effort to chuckle because the comedian imposed on them an uneasy self-awareness. They feel that they are now being judged and have a responsibility to be more supportive of the performer. They also want to escape more chiding from the stage. The whole experience becomes unsatisfying, and the audience can't wait for it to end.

You may never take to the stage at a comedy club, but you will have presentation audiences who do not actively show the interest and support you desire. You crave a smile or two; maybe a nod here and there. Instead, everyone just sits there, looking at you.

No matter how much you crave a few active signs of interest, don't start commenting on the lack of encouraging behavior! Not only will it not help; it is likely to make the situation worse.

First, keep in mind that your audience members may be more tuned in than you realize. I, myself, have a tendency to become still and quiet when I am concentrating on something. If, when I'm in that state, the speaker chides me about my lack of expression, it's annoying. From that point on there is no chance I am going to fully concentrate on the message. I have been made self-conscious when I was, in fact, fully speaker conscious.

Even if you are sure the audience is not with you, don't make an issue of it. Instead, focus your energies on what you might do to encourage more attentiveness.

You might, for example, initiate a dialogue with the audience by pausing and asking for comments. This not only can spark some responsiveness, it can provide you with insight into how your message might be missing the mark.

Focusing on better serving your listeners is going to be far more productive than focusing—and commenting—on how they can better serve you.

Chapter 5 Delivery Strategy

Speak for the Audience

Presenters who affect a casual, conversational style can get thrown off when an audience is large. This is particularly true of speakers who depend on questions and comments to keep them in a conversational mode.

Some speakers will try to remedy this by soliciting participation from the front row. In essence they are turning the people close to them into the smaller audience they prefer. The inappropriateness of this technique should be obvious. It makes the people sitting farther back feel like they are sitting in the cheap seats.

A simple solution is to speak for the audience. I think of it as setting up a faux conversation. The speaker presents some material and then frames a question that someone in the audience could have. *I know when you hear me describe this new system your first thought is "How are we ever going to get it up and running on time?"*

Then, the speaker answers the question. *Well, let me say a few things about how we plan to expedite the transition.*

This technique helps give a big-audience presentation the more intimate feel of a smaller, conversational piece. It sounds interactive even though the speaker is carrying both sides of the conversation.

It's also a good way to raise potential objections audience members may have. If the speaker voices the objection rather than waiting for someone in the audience to do so, the timing and wording of it can be controlled. Instead of trying to respond to "The amount of money you are asking for is way too high!" the speaker can preempt the objection with something more reasonable such as, "Why is the investment we are proposing so significant? Let me explain."

It's always possible to dialogue with your audience, even if you have to carry both sides of the conversation.

Give Them a Chance to Breathe

The curse of being a speech coach is that you analyze every speaker you encounter, even when you are not "on the job," and it's inappropriate. I shamefully confess that this compulsion has even got the better of me at funeral services when the eulogy is being delivered.

What I have noticed with eulogies is that most people instinctively understand that they have to let their audience members breathe. By this, I mean they lighten up at times and say something humorous. After stretches of tearful heaviness, these humorous interludes offer people in the audience a chance to catch their breath.

When you are delivering a heavy message of any kind, it can be as if you have your knee on the collective chest of your audience members. You may not actually be squeezing the air out of them, but it feels like it. At some point you need to let up and give everyone a chance to breathe. Otherwise, they have to find their own relief by tuning you out. It's a matter of self-preservation.

You may, for example, be presenting an analysis of how a team failed to meet customer expectations and lost a big piece of business. Without question, it's important that the team members understand what happened and learn from their mistakes. However, they will stop listening—and stop learning—if you relentlessly pour on the guilt. They can only take so much.

But they need to know they messed up! This can't be just a slap on the wrist.

There is a difference between letting audience members breathe and letting people "off the hook." The objective is not to contradict or negate your own message, but to enable your listeners to stay open and receptive. Ironically, a relentlessly hard message will actually have less effect than one that periodically lightens up. Once you force people to tune you out, nothing you say has impact.

Humor is not the only way to lighten up and let people breathe. In fact, in some instances it would not be advisable. Someone speaking about a tragic accident can, for example, give the audience relief by complimenting heroic actions or going over some procedural issues. Again, the objective is not to do away with the heaviness of the message, but to be sensitive to its potentially suffocating nature.

There is a time to pour it on. There is a time to let up.

End on Time

People complain about it all the time, and presenters just keep doing it.

What am I talking about? I am talking about presenting longer than promised. I'm talking about the 20-minute presentation that inevitably runs for 40 minutes and makes five people late for another meeting.

I once attended an annual luncheon program sponsored by a commercial real estate firm in Denver. There were over five hundred people in attendance. I was so impressed by the level of attendance that I sought out the gentleman who was in charge of planning the event. I asked him how he had managed to get so many busy people to show up. I thought he would say something about the quality of the program, but instead, he said: "People trust us. They know we will start on time and not go even one minute past the ninety minutes scheduled."

He explained that they had learned years earlier that the busiest, most influential members of the commercial real estate community would show up *if* they knew with certainty that their time would be respected. Each executive scheduled to present was allotted seven minutes. If he or she "ran even ten seconds too long it was time to start looking for a new job." Of course, the program also had to be good, but he was adamant that the key to exceptional attendance was time management.

The discontent with overlong presentations is so widespread that the opportunity to make a positive impression by staying on time is tremendous. Almost nobody does it. If you consistently start on time and end on time, it's guaranteed you are going to score points with your audiences.

As a bonus, you will enjoy better attention and participation. People are more willing to contribute with questions and discussion points if they don't have to worry about making a time management problem worse.

If factors beyond your control create the likelihood of running over time, talk to your audience about it. Explain what you still have to cover and determine if they have the time *and* willingness to let you continue. Be willing to graciously stop and make arrangements to get the remaining information to them by other means.

Be unique. Respect people's time.

6
Platform Skills

Know When Your Performance Really Starts

You have been asked to represent the marketing department at a regional sales meeting. Seventy-five of your company's salespeople have gathered at a hotel for a full day of presentations, and your turn in the spotlight is scheduled for 11:00 a.m.

If you are like most presenters, your early-morning attitude is "I can relax for now. I'm not on until eleven." Even though you are in the presentation room, you behave like someone off-stage. You sit in the back corner sending wireless e-mails or reviewing your slides. Maybe you chat with one of the sales managers you know or concentrate on nursing a coffee while leaning against the wall. Whatever you do, you assume the attention will not be on you until 11 a.m. *Then* you will have to focus on how you are being perceived.

What you don't realize is that your performance has already

begun. You are making first impressions. You began to communicate with your audience when you first walked into the room, even if you didn't say anything to anybody. If you exuded poise and confidence, it was noted. If, in contrast, you acted unsure of yourself, that was noted. These impressions became the first installments in the total message your audience members will take away from your participation in the meeting.

As the morning progresses, people are noticing things like how attentive you are to the other presentations. (Are you truly interested in their world?) They note who you talk to and draw conclusions about your status. They look for signs of likeability that may make them more receptive to your marketing message later that morning. The possibilities are many.

People are going to read you just as surely as they read your slides. If you are not aware of this until your first slide goes up, you are late. That ever-important first impression has been made and it's influencing your intended message.

Please understand, I'm not suggesting that you go into some kind of an act the moment you arrive. Your future audience members will read phoniness as sure as they read any other message you communicate. You must always be authentic. But, you also have to be consciously aware that your behavior is sending a message.

If, for example, you are tempted to stay withdrawn and worry about your presentation, consciously snap out of it and go shake a few hands. If your attention is wavering during the early presentations, sit forward in your seat and renew your eye contact with the presenter. As you move around the room checking computer plug-ins or distributing handouts, don't get so task focused that you ignore people. Before you even go in the room, check yourself in a mirror and make sure the first impression you are going to make is not of a sloppy, unaware persona.

Your public speaking message begins as soon as you are in public. It begins long before you face the audience and make your opening comments.

Know when your performance really starts.

Own the Geography

We've talked about owning the time you are given to speak. Something else you should "own" is the geography.

Instead of standing in one place like a tree, take advantage of the available floor space. Move around. Add to the dynamic quality of your speaking style.

Take at least a couple of steps and then stop. Stand comfortably still while you say a few things, and then travel somewhere else in the available geography. Be purposeful about it, not wandering aimlessly or pacing nervously.

Moving in toward your audience is particularly strong. Movement and closeness to the audience project confidence. As I stated in an earlier section, they also enhance a sense of "connectedness."

You can overdo it, of course. Resist the temptation to become a television host, walking deep into the audience. This is awkward for the people in the front rows. It works on TV because one or more people stay on the stage as a point of focus.

If you do venture in a ways, such as when the audience is seated in a horseshoe arrangement, don't stay long. Work your way back to the front so you can again make easy eye contact with everyone.

Movement can also be used to correct or compensate for things. For example, chatty audience members will usually quiet down if you move toward them. Also, people sitting on the far wings of a large audience will feel more included if you occasionally move in their direction. I use movement whenever I catch myself not giving adequate attention to any part of my audience. Instead of just trying to remember to look in that direction, I'll make a point of walking toward those people.

Give it a try the next time you present. Act like you own the geography in the front of the room. Don't feel you have to stay behind the lectern or remain chained to your laptop. If a microphone is needed, ask for a portable one. If you have to advance your own slides, use a remote control.

The payoff will be a more dynamic style.

Include Sign Language

Gesturing is one of the first topics covered in Presentation Skills 101. Yet, even in advanced workshops, someone will say, "I don't know what to do with my hands!" and half the people in the room will nod.

They know the basics—hands out of pockets, up and out, no pointing, etcetera. Yet they still feel awkward. The problem is that they have a limited repertoire of gestures. Their complaint should be "I don't know what *else* to do with my hands."

Have your next presentation videotaped. When you review the tape, push down on the fast-forward button. Your movements will be exaggerated, like you are the star of an old-time, silent film. Most likely you will see that your own repertoire of gestures is limited to two or three movements repeated over and over again.

Some training programs urge speakers to develop several new gestures and rehearse them. These workshops will dedicate a sizeable chunk of time to hand-gesture choreography. I'm sure this helps some people, but it comes with the risk of looking unnatural.

I once attended a college graduation ceremony in Detroit's Cobo Arena. The dean of the college gave the main address and he obviously had choreographed his gesturing. He would talk about looking off to his left, and then, with a half-second delay, hold out his left hand. This would be repeated with the right hand. It was a gallant effort, but the deliberateness of it was distracting.

The best way to add some variety to your hand gestures—and not look artificial—is to do some rough pantomiming.

You might start with your open hands close together and spread them wider as you talk about the expanding scope of a project. Or, you might incrementally lower your hand as you talk about the steady drop in interest rates. A strong partnership may be symbolized by your clasped hands. You might even take an imaginary swing at a ball as you talk about the marketing department's home run.

This kind of gesturing spontaneously adds to your repertoire of gestures. The spontaneity, in turn, ensures variety. I particularly like this approach because it adds a strong visual element to your speaking; your audience hears *and* sees the point you are making. This helps your visually oriented audience members.

Of course, you don't want to overdo it. Anything overdone is distracting. You're not auditioning for street theatre. You just want to increase the variety of your gestures, and do it in a way that adds to the dynamic quality of your speaking style.

Develop a habit of rough pantomiming and you will no longer have to worry about what to do with your hands.

Ground Yourself When Necessary

There was a time when speakers were taught to either gesture or let their hands hang loosely by their side. The goal was to avoid nervous hand movements that either communicated a lack of ease or distracted the audience.

Few people can comfortably let their hands hang by their side. It makes them feel uneasy. A much better alternative is to touch the fingertips of one hand to something like a nearby table or lectern. Instantly you feel comfortably grounded. It's as if we humans are electrical and need a grounding wire.

Many people have told me that this simple tip alone did away with the chronic anxiety they had over what to do with their hands. They no longer fidget, wring their hands, or play with jewelry. Instead of awkwardly holding their hands behind their back or clutched in front, they stand relaxed and poised. As a bonus, any problem they had with nervous feet also stopped.

With a little bit of thought ahead of time, you can often give yourself a grounding point by moving a piece of furniture. I'll drag a table to the front of the room if there isn't one already there. If the tables are too low for my height, I'll see if I can position a chair so that I'll be able to occasionally walk over to it and rest my hand on the back of it. This chair technique works best when you are presenting at the head of a conference table and no one needed the closest seat. Of course, if there is a lectern you are all set even if you didn't plan to stand behind it. You can stand to the side of it and rest your hand.

Some presenters find that holding something, like a pen, is all they need. The trouble with that technique is that they unconsciously start playing with the object. If it's a ballpoint pen, they will repeatedly click it. If it's their notes, they'll roll them up in a tube and wave them around. If it's a laser pointer, they will spin it around on their fingers. They feel more grounded, but their audience is distracted.

Of course, you are probably wondering what to do if you ever have to stand out in the middle of an empty stage. First, see if you can have something like a stool or music stand set on the stage. Their purpose as your grounding point can be disguised with a glass of water set on the stool and a few unnecessary pages of notes on the stand. If these options are not available, then try touching the bottom of your jacket. Or, if you decide it is worth the risk of holding something, ask for a handheld wireless microphone.

A well-grounded speaker is a physically calm speaker.

Look Them in the Eye

When you finish a presentation, your audience members should each feel like you spoke directly to them. This should be true even if there were 20 people in the room. It's essential if you want to make a strong personal connection.

You're only going to make this happen if you really look at people. You don't fixate on your slides. You don't focus on the back wall. You don't stare off into space. *And* (please!) you don't follow the ever-popular advice to look just over people's heads if you are nervous.

You really look at people.

I'm not suggesting you stare. That makes people uncomfortable. Besides, they say staring means either aggression or affection, and you're not looking for a fight or a date.

Many presentation skills courses say you should finish a thought with one person before moving on to someone else. I must have long thoughts because that has always felt too long to me. Look at somebody just long enough that you both feel the connection (two or three seconds) and then move on.

Some presenters protest that they can't think and look at

people at the same time. If that describes you, you're going to have to plan and rehearse your presentations enough that the material comes to your mind easily. Regularly looking away during a one-on-one conversation is normal and expected, but in a group presentation you need to be looking at someone most of the time.

Work at being democratic with your eye contact. Include everyone. You'll be tempted to favor the people who appear most receptive to your message, but you need to connect with the others as well. I once taught a class that included the perfect audience member. This individual eagerly concentrated on every speaker—smiling, nodding, laughing; she was great. Every class member who gave a presentation ended up just making eye contact with her and ignoring everybody else.

Another temptation that can restrict your eye contact is the presence of an important decision maker. Because you know this person has the last word in accepting or rejecting your proposal, you present just to him or her. This "decision-maker eye contact" is dangerous. It may seem smart at the moment, but nothing good can ultimately come from making the other audience members feel neglected. I can almost guarantee that one of them has influence with the decision maker that you are not aware of.

What do you do if the audience is big? Look toward groups of people. In a large audience people will be farther away. Your eye contact toward a group will be perceived as personal eye contact by every individual in the group.

Again, the objective is to make everybody feel like you noticed them and you spoke to them. The key is eye contact.

Develop a Better Voice

Once when I was waiting for an elevator at a client's office tower, a woman ran up to me and said, "I did what you told me to do!" Although I recognized her as someone who had been in one of my workshops, I could not remember what I had told her. My expression obviously gave me away.

"Oh, you know," she continued. "I spoke so softly no one could hear me. You suggested I get some voice lessons. So I did! Now when I whisper, people can hear me clear across the room. And you know what? I'm so much more confident!" And with that she ran off to join a coworker.

I was so pleased to hear that someone had taken me up on that particular piece of advice. I've suggested voice lessons to many people over the years and they typically do nothing about it. I work primarily with business people, and the idea of voice lessons sounds terribly un-business-like to them. *Actors get voice lessons. Stage performers get voice lessons. Business people don't get voice lessons.* The resistance is even stronger with science or technology people.

I find this attitude so frustrating. Your voice plays a critical role in determining how successful you are as a presenter. It directly affects how much people listen to you and what kind of an image you project.

If, for example, you speak in a monotone—as many presenters do—an audience will tune you out. Ask a group of people how long they will listen to such a voice and the typical answer is "two minutes."

Weak voices also discourage listening. People tire of trying to hear someone—unless, of course, that someone is reading their rich uncle's will.

Confidence and enthusiasm are communicated, to a great extent, by a person's voice. If we hear you speak in a clear, strong, and animated voice, we're more likely to take notice of both you and your message.

Most people would agree with these points, so why are so few inclined to do anything about having a better voice? Part of it is the "only performers get voice lessons" belief. Another reason is that people tend to believe their voice is a fixed part of who they are—like their height or eye color. *I have my mother's voice. Everybody in our family talks this way. I've always been quiet.*

Sure, there are elements of a voice that are physically determined. But an amazing amount of our voice quality is determined by how we use what we physically have.

For example, do some reading on voice quality and you soon learn that one of the biggest determiners of how we sound is how we breathe. When people learn how to breathe in a way that better supports their voice, they sound significantly better. I suspect the voice coach who helped my soft-spoken class participant focused a good deal on her breathing.

I sought out a voice coach early in my career because I was a mumbler. Although I came from a family of mumblers, I was not going to accept it as my destiny.

People don't think twice about "getting a couple of lessons" to improve their performance in a sport or hobby. Yet they will go an entire career without getting help for a voice that detracts from their performance as a communicator. They have a weakness where they could have a strength, but they don't do anything about it. If you suspect your voice could use some improvement, be one of those rare people who does something about it. A relatively small investment in time and money will pay off big.

Sound Like You Care

It is amazing how many people say they hate listening to a monotone voice, yet present with one themselves. I run into this phenomenon all the time.

Some need voice lessons, but many others have bought into a couple of myths.

The first myth says that serious professionalism requires a dispassionate delivery. A voice that gives no evidence of feeling is the voice of reason.

The second myth says that a dispassionate voice offers protection. A presenter who doesn't sound "up" about an idea cannot be embarrassingly brought "down" by a critical audience member.

Both these beliefs are flawed.

Though reason can sound absent when someone is acting highly emotional, it's not compromised by a reasonable level of enthusiasm.

And, the danger of being brought low comes with enthusiasm

not supported by good content—not by enthusiasm *for* good content.

It would be bad enough if these myths just led to a boring delivery, but the damage is worse. They rob a presenter of the sound of conviction. If you want to convince an audience about something, you have to sound convinced yourself.

If you want an audience to care about something, you have to sound like you care.

I'm not talking about an over-the-top vocal performance. This is not about sounding like a high-energy, wildly animated, motivational speaker. It's about sounding like you care about your subject. Your audience members need to hear in your voice that you give a darn. They are not going to get into something any more than you sound like you're into it.

It should not be an act. It should be the real you talking with real conviction.

Will it guarantee support? No, not necessarily. In fact, the reaction may be the sound of heartfelt opposition. But even negative engagement is far preferable to apathy.

Do you want others to care? Then sound like you do.

Give Voice to Your Characters

When you include anecdotal material in a presentation, you typically introduce your audience to characters. For example, you may describe a certain irate customer as part of a story about customer service. *Awhile back I had an angry customer call me at least six times on the same day. Every time I thought we had his problem solved, he would call back with a new demand.*

If you tell your stories the way most presenters do, you describe these characters' involvement the same way a reporter would. *He told me that an equal exchange was not good enough. He wanted us to give him an upgraded model in place of the one that was giving him trouble. I told him that was not a decision I could make.*

This is a perfectly reasonable way to tell what was said in a personal encounter. There is, however, a way to make your story more engaging to an audience.

If you actually act out the dialogue by playing the characters, your audience members will go from learning what happened to vicariously experiencing the event. It will be as if they are there, witnessing what is being said. This gives your storytelling more impact.

I'm not suggesting you put on a one-person stage show. I just want you to give some voice to the characters.

Then he calls me back and says (*switch to gruff voice*): "I've changed my mind. I want you to give me a better model than the one I'm returning."

I couldn't believe it. I said (*switch tone to careful politeness*): "Sir, I will have to talk to my boss about this. I'm not authorized to make such a decision."

If you throw in some appropriate facial expressions and for

a couple of seconds pantomime being on a phone, the effect will be even stronger.

Again, you don't want to overdo it and pretend you are acting on Broadway. Just a small amount of acting is enough.

Speakers who do this well give voice to characters throughout their presentations. They flow in and out of character so smoothly their audience members are not consciously aware of the technique. They are too engrossed to notice.

The next time you include something anecdotal, give it a try. Experiment. Your storytelling will take on a new dimension.

Pause for Effect

I once listened to a preacher pause after making an important point, and then say under his breath, but loud enough for everybody to hear: "Pause for effect." His intent was to get a laugh, but he was touching upon an important principle in public speaking: Strong speakers pause.

A pause emphasizes the last thing you said. It gives it a chance to sink in with your listeners. In addition, it builds anticipation for the next thing you are going to say.

Pauses can also signal a change in thought or direction. Imagine trying to read a book with no paragraphs or chapters, just a continuous string of sentences, page after page. It would be exhausting to read. You would toss it aside unfinished. Without pauses, a presentation can have that same run-together quality.

As valuable as they are, pauses come hard to many presenters. They are uncomfortable with silence. As soon as they finish one point, they *have* to start the next point. The slightest pause feels awkwardly long.

Any pause you take in your delivery is not as long as it seems. Prove it to yourself in your next presentation. Pause a few times and then, afterward, ask a couple of audience members if your pauses were too long. Not only will they say "no," they will probably say they don't know what you're talking about.

If you have not been good about pausing in the past, it will take some effort for a while. Find a couple of suitable points in each presentation and mark your notes with a "P" or some other simple reminder mark. When you practice, practice the pauses. Over time "pausing for effect" will become second nature.

Being an effective speaker includes moments when you don't speak.

Reference the Screen, Not Your Laptop

Back in the days of 35mm slide shows, it was common for presenters to gesture toward the projected image as they spoke. Now it is common to see presenters ignoring the main screen, preferring to look down at their laptops.

It is not surprising this has become a standard practice. It eliminates the need to keep turning away from the audience to look at the screen. Presenters only have to glance down to check on the next point.

As easy and natural as it is, I have observed two problems.

The first problem is that those quick glances down at the laptop turn into long stares. Presenters become entranced with the images on their laptop. They lose audience eye contact for extended periods of time.

The second problem is more subtle. I've noticed that the language of presenters changes when they are intent on looking at their own private screen. They are less likely to reference the slides by saying things like "as you can see on this slide" or "as you will notice from the graph." It's as if they stop seeing the slides as a common point of reference and view them solely as their notes. The result is a vague feeling of disconnect between the speaker and the audience.

The connection with your audience is going to be better if you maintain the feeling that you are studying the slides together. *As we look at this graph of average sales, it becomes clear that the employees who receive advanced training generate higher volumes.* This inclusive language is going to flow more naturally if you are, in fact, looking at the same screen the audience members are looking at.

The key to not turning your back on the audience is to get close to the screen. Then you just need to slightly pivot in order to see the screen and gesture toward your slide.

To make sure you can stay close to the screen regardless of where your laptop is plugged in, use a remote control. There are several on the market that work with a radio beam that transmits to a small device you plug into your laptop's USB port. These work the best because you don't have to point at your laptop or worry about a piece of furniture blocking the transmission.

By the way, if you were not aware of it, your best positioning is to your audience's left of the screen. When people read left to right, their eyes automatically refocus back toward the left when they are finished reading. You, as the presenter, want to be there on the left when they look back. Of course, if you are presenting in Arabic or Hebrew, you will want to be on the other side of the screen.

7

Language Use

Lose the "I'm Excited" Line

I'm on a mission. I'm determined to get the executives I coach to stop saying, "I'm excited."

I'm excited about this plan. I'm excited about the new direction we've set. I'm excited about this great team we've assembled. I'm excited about what we've accomplished. I'm excited. I'm excited. I'm excited.

Sales and marketing people are apparently the most excited. It's part of their introduction. "Hi. My name is Ralph and I'm excited."

Some of them say "I'm excited" so much you have to fear for their health. I have visions of whole management teams on the verge of heart attacks from extended overexcitement.

It is a totally worn-out, overused phrase that is no longer

credible. When *everybody* is expressing excitement about *everything*, audiences cannot be expected to believe it. *Yeah, yeah, yeah, I know, you are sooo excited.*

I understand the motivation. Speakers want the audience to enthusiastically buy in to the message. They intuitively know this will not happen unless they themselves project enthusiasm. After all, no audience is going to get charged up if the speaker comes across less than excited. Enthusiasm breeds enthusiasm.

So, speakers simply announce that they are excited. What could be easier?

Nothing could be easier. Also, nothing could be less effective in communicating excitement or enthusiasm.

True enthusiasm does not need to be announced. People recognize it. They instinctively pick up on the speaker's animated behavior and voice.

If your audience naturally picks up on your enthusiasm— *Boy, you're really into this*—it will be far more credible than if you announce, "I'm excited."

Retire Your Favorite Word or Phrase

In addition to losing the "I'm excited" line, I'd like you to search out and retire your favorite word or phrase.

This word or phrase has worked its way into your vocabulary and spread like a computer virus. You say it over and over again without realizing it. The danger is that it will become so prevalent the people you talk to will become distracted by it. In fact, it may already have reached that point—and you are the only one who doesn't know it.

I've mentioned this phenomenon to workshop participants and often they will start talking about an executive in their company who says the same thing over and over, ad nauseam. They laugh and roll their eyeballs. They compare results from the times they have counted the offending word or phrase. *I swear he said it two hundred times at the last management review!* All I can think is: "That poor guy. He undoubtedly thinks his forceful message is the thing they remember most." Instead he impressed them with the 128 different ways he could use the word "basically."

"Basically," by the way, is one of the most popular habit words being used these days. I refer to its popularity as "basically disease." *We basically put together a long-term plan. It doesn't address all the possible issues, but it's basically strong.*

Another favorite, popular with young people, is "like." *Like, we didn't know what to do. So when he told us to leave, we, like, said, "Fine."* We have some friends whose daughter says "like" at least five to six times per minute. I've been thinking of betting her 20 bucks she can't talk for one minute without saying it. That would be the easiest 20 dollars I ever earned.

You may think you don't have a favorite word or phrase, but you do. We all do. I thought I was free of any such word until an associate of mine sat in on a workshop I was conducting. She told me afterward that I used the word "little" constantly. I refused to believe her. Why would I use the word "little" all the time? I might say a few too many uhhms and aahhs, but not "little"—or so I thought, until I listened to myself lecture the next day. I was miniaturizing the whole world! *I'm going to talk a little bit about handling questions. Then we'll practice a little. I want you to get good at using some techniques that will make you a little more effective with presentations you do.*

So far, I've managed a 50% reduction in my use of "little." I need to make more progress as soon as possible so I can work on eliminating another word habit. My wife has informed me that I say "that sort of thing" all the time. I need to get that cured since I really don't like that sort of thing.

To get rid of a word or phrase habit, you have to find out what it is and get to the point that you can hear yourself saying it. Awareness is 80% of the battle. Listening to your own voice-mail messages is one technique for gaining awareness. Tape recording your participation in a meeting is another. Of course, if your self-esteem can handle it, you can always ask someone you know if they have heard you saying the same thing over and over.

If you don't make much progress toward a self-cure, ask a friend, family member, or work associate to point it out whenever you say your favorite word or phrase. This usually leads to quick progress, since you can't stand the nagging. Kids are the best accomplices in this effort as they have no sense of when they should back off and leave you alone. They are relentless. Of course, you should not let them push you to the point of child abuse.

Keeping your vocabulary free of repetitive word usage requires a lifelong commitment. New words and phrases will always be trying to attach themselves to you. Stay alert and you can catch them before they become engrained in your speech pattern.

Don't Lose Them with Your Idioms

At the height of the tech boom of the late 90s, I found myself teaching a presentation skills workshop at the American headquarters of a German software company.

Several participants in the workshop had recently arrived from Germany for a rotation in the American offices. As I chatted with them before the class, I quickly concluded language would not be a problem. Their English was excellent.

So, it surprised me when they placed electronic translators on the tables next to their name tents. Looking like miniature laptop computers, these devices enable a user to type in a word or phrase from one language and learn how the same thing would be said in another language.

I decided they just wanted to have the ability to check something before they spoke.

Instead, they frequently typed into the translators when I was talking. They clearly could not understand everything I was saying no matter how simple I tried to make my language.

What was the problem?!?

I stopped the class and asked.

It turned out to be my frequent use of idioms common to

American English. These individuals had learned what I would call "textbook" English, not idiomatic American English.

The dictionary definition of an idiom is "a fixed distinctive expression whose meaning cannot be deduced from the combined meanings of the actual words." (Encarta Dictionary: English)

So, if I said we would be "*breaking* at 10 a.m.," or would "*knock off* for lunch at noon," they were not sure what I was saying. They were completely lost during my course description when I said they would be learning how to deal with audience members who were *stage hogs* (i.e., people who want constant attention). The electronic translators told them I was referring to pigs.

Aware of the problem, I did my best to eliminate idioms. I couldn't do it. For every idiom I succeeded in eliminating, two more came out of my mouth before I realized it.

The more I tried to weed out the idioms (an idiom) by running through my head (another idiom) what I wanted to say first, the more trouble I ran into (yet, another). By the end of the day I had not only failed to eliminate idioms; I had a major headache.

Subsequent research revealed that native speakers of any language speak a version of that language that is extensively idiomatic. Although this makes the language colorful and vibrant, it also makes it difficult for non-native speakers to understand.

What is the solution?

If you are presenting in your native language to people who have not been living in your country long enough to learn the idioms, make sure you use slides and/or handouts. When we create slides and handouts we tend to be less idiomatic. Also, creating materials in advance gives us an opportunity to edit out idioms that make it past the first draft.

This problem demands attention. You cannot count on people asking you what words and phrases mean. Sometimes they will, but most of the time they will quietly listen with the hope that context will reveal enough of the meaning later.

Did he really say he opened a can of worms? What does that mean? Does it refer to the unexpected problem he is now talking about?

Catch yourself when you can and immediately follow with a non-idiomatic version of what you just said. *We hit a home run with this project. We were very successful.* But don't trust that you will faithfully interpret most of your idioms; you won't even notice them. Deal with them in advance.

Eliminate Unnecessary Qualifiers

There are times when you *have* to qualify what you are saying.

If there is any chance of legal action, it is a good idea to tell your audience members that "past returns are not indicative of future returns" or their "actual results may differ."

It may be necessary to qualify when negotiating support. *We can meet the earlier deadline, if the budget is increased.*

And, at times, you simply have to soften the edges of a message. *Although we strongly propose strategy changes, we realize you have more experience in this market.*

When it's necessary to qualify, do so.

But, when it's not necessary, don't qualify away your authority.

How does this happen? Well, imagine yourself presenting to a management group. You are proposing a new initiative and requesting a large budget to fund it. After making a strong case you conclude your presentation with: "I think this is an investment we should make. I think it has a great deal of potential."

Will the managers approve your big budget? Not likely. Why should they? After all, you only "think" it will work. You are asking them to confidently invest in your plan when you, yourself, sound unsure of it.

My experience is that even the most confident presenters will undermine themselves with unnecessary qualifiers. The inclination is particularly strong at the end of a presentation. At the point of decision, after making a strong case, they will suddenly hedge. It's an instinctive urge, a compulsive need to leave some room for possible failure.

In reality, it buys no insurance. When did you ever hear someone react to a failed plan by reminding everyone that the author "only *thought* it would work"? If your proposal fails, you own the failure, just like you would have hoped to own any success.

Does this mean you should pound the table while loudly guaranteeing things? No, not at all. Just leave out the unnecessary qualifiers. *This plan addresses the key objectives while staying within the budget. We urge its implementation.*

You don't want to invite resistance by coming across certain of something everyone knows can't be certain. You just want to avoid inadvertently undermining the audience's confidence in your message.

The next time you are in a meeting, listen to yourself. Do you habitually qualify? *It's probably not a bad idea. I think it might work. Maybe we can make the change next week.* If you hear this tendency in your language, start weeding out the qualifiers. Over time your language will take on a more confident character. Then you will be able to trust it more in presentations. You won't finish a big proposal on a weak note with "I think it might work. I hope you do, too."

Translate Lingo

Even if you don't speak a foreign language, you are multilingual. The organization you work for has a language all its own. So does your career specialty, and any other "world" you inhabit from a religious affiliation to sports.

The longer you speak these languages, the more a part of you they become. As long as everybody you are talking to speaks the same language, it works. In fact, communication improves and you build your credibility as an insider.

Problems develop when you are speaking to people who don't know the language. If it were a case of you trying to speak

English to people without English proficiency, you would be totally aware of the problem and committed to making sure there is a translation. But when you are speaking an organizational or career specialty language, you typically don't realize there is a communication problem.

You may, for example, use acronyms in place of full job titles as you explain how a project team is being staffed. You talk about the PS and ICM working hand in hand, and the finance people sitting in front of you have no idea you are talking about the Procurement Specialist and Inventory Control Manager.

Then you go on to emphasize the advantages of this arrangement for ensuring forward placement of parts and equipment. "Forward placement?" Do they know you mean the stocking of parts and equipment in overseas warehouses, close to where they may be needed in the event of an emergency? Maybe they're not familiar with the term because their organization calls it something else.

An executive once told me he solves the lingo problem by having his kids listen to his presentations and learning from them what they didn't understand. Others have told me they enlist the aid of their spouses. I can see where either strategy would work if you were facing general audiences that included people totally unfamiliar with the subject matter (example: community members learning about the reclamation of a nearby toxic waste dump). If your kids or spouse understand what you are saying, you can be confident that you are using generally understood language.

I would not use the kids/spouse review strategy when you are going to be presenting to people who are knowledgeable in your industry and only unfamiliar with your specialty. They will understand—and expect—terminology your family members don't understand.

If possible, get someone who is representative of your audience to look over your slides. This may not help with everything you say, but it will at least reduce the number of unknown terms. People in your own department or specialty are not the best reviewers since they speak the same language you do.

You can also, at the start of your presentation, invite your audience members to ask for clarification if you use an unfamiliar term. They will be less self-conscious about asking since you already suggested it may be necessary and you took responsibility for it in advance.

Finally, don't hesitate to explain a term or repeat something with different wording if you have just said something using potentially unfamiliar lingo. You don't have to make a big deal out of it. Interpret and move on.

8
Q & A

Ask Who Has the First Question

If you want uncomfortable silence when asking for questions, use the standard line: "Are there any questions?" Most audience members will not respond.

They don't respond because they interpret what you are saying to mean "Does anyone need help understanding the material?" This is what it meant when they were going to school.

They will not ask questions because they don't want to give the impression they are having trouble grasping what is being said.

I encountered this phenomenon when I went back to college after being away for a few years. I was less intimidated by professors and more motivated than I had previously been. In addition, I was now married and my wife and I were living on her income. My desire to learn, and justify my wife's sacrifice, trumped any concern about not appearing smart. When a professor asked if there were any questions, and I had one, my hand went up. Time and again others in the room would react by announcing that they, too, had the same question. *Yeah, I didn't get it either.* If I hadn't said something, they would have stayed quiet. They were not going to take the chance of looking like the only person in the room who was not keeping up.

When you give a presentation, you can count on the same thing happening. Some people will ask questions no matter what, but many others will hang back and not say anything. They don't want to appear to be having trouble.

You can avoid this problem by asking for questions differently. Instead of asking if anyone has a question, ask who has the first question. *I've covered quite a bit of material and I am sure there are some questions. Who has the first one?* The message you send then is that questions are expected, and the only thing you are checking for is who is going to start—not who doesn't comprehend the material.

Change the way you ask for questions and avoid both awkward silences *and* people leaving the room with unanswered questions.

Don't Take Premature Ownership

You give what you think is an eloquent answer to a question, only to hear, "That's interesting, but that's not what I asked you." Now *there* is a line that can make you feel two inches tall.

Most often the problem is that you took ownership of the question prematurely.

Before you have any responsibility for the answer to a question, the person doing the asking has responsibility for the question. Regardless of the pressure on you to be responsive, you have the right to a clearly articulated, understandable question.

There is something about public speaking that causes even the most careful people to be in a hurry to give answers. They will begin answering the second a questioner stops talking, even if the question was vague and confusing. They guess at what is being asked and then start talking. This is what I call taking ownership of a question prematurely.

Fight the urge to compulsively answer.

I used to play softball in a church league. Some of the pitchers in this league could not throw a ball straight if their life depended on it. And yet, they were successful. Batters would get so impatient with the bad pitches, they would take a wild swing and either miss completely or send an easy-to-catch blooper to one of the infielders. Few had the discipline to hold out for a decent pitch.

Just like a batter needs a decent pitch to swing at, you need—and deserve—a decent, understandable question to respond to. If you take a "swing" at what you think is being asked, you're likely to miss. Then, ironically, it will appear that *you* are performing badly when, in fact, it was the *questioner* who did not communicate well.

Often, the key to giving a quality answer is first insisting on a quality question. Don't be shy about asking for clarification. *I'm not sure I'm clear on what you are asking. Could you repeat your question? I want to make sure I answer you correctly.*

Remember, a question belongs to the questioner until you understand it. Then—and only then—is it appropriate for you to take ownership and the responsibility to answer that goes with it.

Answer in a Full Thought

Do you ever watch news conferences on TV? The view is of some government official standing behind a lectern. Reporters you cannot see fire off questions you cannot hear. The best you can do is guess at the questions based on the answers.

Something similar happens in presentations. A person in the front row asks a question that people in the back row cannot hear. Someone might call out, "We didn't hear the question!" More often, the people in the back just follow along as best as they can by listening to the presenter.

Presenters rarely notice the problem because they are totally focused on answering the question. This preoccupation with answering also explains why they usually don't remember the standard advice to repeat questions.

You do not *have* to remember to repeat questions *if* you have the habit of answering in a full sentence. If someone asks, "What is the budget?" you don't just say, "Ten thousand dollars." You say: "There is ten thousand dollars in the budget." If they want to know how long a promotion is going to run, you don't just say, "Two weeks." You say, "The promotion is going to run for two weeks."

When you answer in a full sentence, the question is built right into your answer. If someone didn't hear the question, no problem; they know what was asked based on your answer.

This full-sentence habit is particularly useful when you're asked follow-up questions by the same person. Your tendency will be to focus only on that one person and to give shorter and shorter responses. *No, I don't think so. Well, yes, that might be true. I can't say for sure.* Others in the room will feel like they are listening to one side of a telephone conversation unless you keep responding in full sentences. Then everyone can follow along even if they can't hear the persistent audience member.

Practice this full-sentence technique in everyday telephone conversations and meetings. When it becomes a habit, you will be one of those rare presenters who never leaves anyone wondering what the question was.

Answer and Move On

Blues musicians sometimes play false endings. They stretch out what sounds like the last…few…notes in a tune; pause briefly; and then start playing again. They may do this multiple times in one musical piece. Embarrassed audience members clap prematurely.

Music critics will praise one band for playing a false ending, but criticize another band for doing the same thing. They like it if the additional playing "adds something." They don't like it if the tune was complete and should have ended.

Presenters "play" false endings. You hear them during the question and answer period.

The presenter takes a question and answers it. Every indication is that it's time for another question. But, no, the speaker picks back up with additional thoughts about the last question. Raised hands hesitate and go back down.

Adding on to an answer can be a good thing. It can provide clarification. It can answer future questions people might have. Often, however, false endings make speakers appear uncertain or prone to ramble.

Most of the time, you will make the best impression if you give a concise answer and move on to the next question. If someone wants you to elaborate, they can ask you to. Otherwise, you keep the Q & A period moving along while demonstrating confidence in the adequacy of your answers.

Answer to Everyone

When someone in the audience asks a question, most presenters respond with their attention focused only on that individual and no one else. It's the natural thing to do.

A rarely seen, stronger speaking style is to answer to the whole audience. You begin and end focused on the questioner, but during your answer you also give eye contact to other people in the audience. This maintains your connection with the whole audience.

This answer-to-everyone style is rare because it runs counter to human nature. I recall going to a meeting at our church after a day of teaching presentation skills. Our pastor asked me about a project, and I directed my entire answer to him. Even after having just taught others to look around when answering, I, too, maintained laser-like focus on my questioner.

You will never be faulted for answering only to the person who asked the question. After all, it's the norm. But, if you practice answering to the whole audience, you will project a more commanding style. You will be seen to have more of that subtle quality called "presence."

A helpful tip is to address the audience as a lead-in to your answer. *Okay. That's something I'm sure many of you are wondering about. How are we going to make sure we finish this project on time? Let me talk about the timetable.* By addressing the whole group, you automatically feel more comfortable looking around as you answer.

Please notice that a repetition of the question is included. This is a good idea because it makes looking around seem more natural. Once you have told the whole audience the question, it follows that you would tell the whole audience the answer.

Do you have to do this with every question you get? No. You can make a good impression even if you only use it with some of the questions. Also, there will be times when you may decide it's ill-advisable to look around, such as when the CEO asks you a question that begins with "I want to know why…"

Try it out the next time you are in a meeting, or even just talking with friends at a restaurant. You'll be struck by how hard it is to do. But keep at it and you'll develop an ability that few presenters have.

Sneak in a Forgotten Point

It's usually not a good idea to admit to an audience that you forgot something. *Oh! I almost forgot. I need to tell you about a change we are making to the reporting structure.*

When people realize you have had a lapse in memory, they wonder how many other things you may have forgotten. Can they be sure you have not left out something else that will prove to be critical?

Sometimes you can weave in a point when you remember it. Other times you can't because it would be too out of place. If you wedged it in, the flow of your message would be disrupted and it would be obvious that you had forgotten it earlier. When this is the case, wait until you reach the question and answer period.

By its very nature, the question and answer period jumps around within the overall subject matter. Questions don't have to flow naturally from what preceded them. This gives you the flexibility to introduce a forgotten point without having it feel out of place. You do this by asking yourself about it.

Instead of crossing your fingers and hoping someone in the audience will bring it up, you can introduce it as "a question one of you might have." *One question I'm sure somebody has is "How are we going to find money to pay for this additional production?" Let me say a few words about that.* You had originally planned to talk about supplemental funding during your presentation, but you forgot. Now, you can smoothly address it in response to a question. The fact that you yourself asked the question is not important.

We all forget material. It's the nature of public speaking. The challenge is to overcome a lapse in memory without raising doubts about the completeness of your message. The ask-yourself-a-question tactic works well.

9
Challenging Audiences

Work It Out Before the Presentation

The best time to deal with troublesome audience members is before they become troublesome audience members. If you can meet with them in advance and negotiate a peace treaty, your presentation will go better.

Sure, I know, it's impressive if you deftly handle them in the presentation. But no matter how well you handle it, the tone of your presentation will not be as good as it could have been without the trouble.

I used to be responsible for a monthly presentation to a business association board of directors in Texas. There was a gentleman on the board who was determined to oppose me in every meeting. He was loud and animated by nature, so he could put on quite a performance. I typically did well responding in a professional manner, but he still succeeded in creating an atmosphere of conflict that hampered the association's effectiveness.

I eventually learned that I had to meet with this man the day before every meeting. I was young at the time, and it irked me that I had to give him special attention. But, I had to admit that it reduced the amount of trouble significantly. We would debate issues over coffee and, even if we agreed to disagree, he was more cooperative during the actual board meeting.

When you were a kid your mother taught you to stay away from troublemakers. It was good advice. But if you are scheduled to do a presentation, and you have reason to believe there will be trouble, you may want to seek out the malcontents and try negotiating a peace treaty.

Trouble that doesn't occur is better than trouble well handled.

Negotiate Rules

Well-managed meetings typically have ground rules. The group has agreed to limit sidebar conversations or to keep cell phones turned off. Other rules may include a strict adherence to the agenda or participation by everyone.

When these rules have been agreed to at the beginning of a meeting, they help stop a lot of unproductive behavior. If, for example, a couple of people start having a private conversation, they can be politely reminded of the no-sidebar-conversations rule, and it doesn't come across like they are being arbitrarily picked on.

If a meeting with ground rules includes a presentation, the presenter benefits. If the meeting facilitator is someone other than the presenter, it's even better. When disruptive or non-productive behavior starts, the facilitator can interrupt just long enough for a rule reminder, and then the presenter can get right back on track.

Two suggestions make all the difference in the successful use of ground rules.

1. Establish the rules at the start of the meeting, before unproductive behavior happens. If they are established after the behavior has begun, it is too obvious who is the target of the rule.

2. When those in attendance are part of an ongoing group, make establishment of the rules a group activity. When everyone has a say, the rules are better kept.

If you feel the word "rules" smacks too much of authority or control, don't use it. Talk of "guidelines" or "suggestions." *Before we get started I'd like to suggest some guidelines that will help us get through everything we have to cover in a reasonable amount of time.*

Just the act of getting people to think about what is and isn't acceptable behavior can do wonders. They become more conscious of how they need to act as meeting participants and presentation audience members.

Ask for a Hearing

Sometimes you can't concentrate on *the* troublemaker because the whole audience promises to be trouble. There's a room full of disgruntled employees, shareholders, or community activists wound up and ready to gang up on poor little you.

My hope is you never have to be in a situation like this. I can tell you from experience that it is not pleasant. Anger feeds on anger to the point that normally reasonable people become quite unreasonable.

If, unfortunately, you ever do have to face the mob, know that you can usually get ten uninterrupted minutes if you ask for them. *I know you have come here unhappy about the latest company proposal. But, if you will give me ten minutes to explain our position, I promise I will then stop and we will have a candid discussion about your concerns.*

If you ask for a hearing in this manner, most audiences— no matter how mad they are—will give you ten minutes to make your case. Notice, however, that their cooperation is predicated upon your promise to listen to what they have to say when your ten minutes is up. You have to make this promise *and* keep it.

These ten minutes are particularly precious if miscommu- nication, misunderstandings, or unfounded rumor have contributed to the bad atmosphere. You have a chance to set the record straight and make your case in an organized way.

This ten-minute grace period will not guarantee a peaceful meeting. The protests may start right at the ten-minute mark.

But you will be in a better position than you otherwise would have been.

Never Let Them See You Sweat

We have all been there. Someone in the audience launches a verbal attack on the presenter. *This is just another flavor-of-the-month gimmick that won't accomplish anything!*

In unison the whole room stops breathing. *Oh boy, here we go. What's going to happen? Is this going to get ugly?*

All eyes and ears turn to the presenter. Will he crumble? Will she lash back? Everyone is watching to see how the presenter reacts.

Think back to the last time you were in an audience when this happened. I'll bet you can still remember how the presenter reacted—*even* if you can't remember what the specific issue was.

If the presenter remained calm and relaxed, you recall being impressed. *The guy had his act together. He showed a lot of confidence.*

If the presenter acted anxious or defensive, you remember not being impressed.

When you are a presenter and you face a challenge from the audience, do your best to stay calm and show no signs of defensiveness.

I know, I know, this is easier said than done, but it is crucial to your success. Never forget that the impression you make may even be more important than your answer.

A calm reaction reflects well on you and has the bonus value of increasing the audience's confidence in your message. After all, if you're not bothered by an attack, you obviously must believe your message will stand up to criticism. If you have that much confidence in it, maybe they should, too.

If you want to impress people when your message is being criticized, remember the old TV commercial: Never let them see you sweat.

Test the Antagonist's Support

In one of my first jobs I often spoke to audiences that included unhappy people. I was charged with presenting marketing plans to business association members, and any number of them could be antagonistic.

Just to add an extra degree of challenge, each presentation had to end with a vote. Whatever plans I was proposing could only be implemented if a majority of the association members approved them. Vocal antagonists could do more than just make the job of presenting difficult; they could sour the vote.

I learned many valuable lessons in that pressure-cooker environment. One of the most important ones was the need to quickly test if an antagonist truly represents the audience.

People challenging a presenter depend on the impression that they are speaking for many others. They want you to believe that they are the voice of the silent majority sitting around them. This gives them power.

Before I knew better, I went along with this. I readily assumed anyone challenging me had spokesperson status. That is what they wanted me to think, and I did.

One day it hit me. *Wait a minute. Is this person who is condemning my plan really speaking for the whole room? Is it really me versus everybody else? Do I know for sure?*

From that day on I started checking with the rest of the audience. If John Doe declared that the kind of special events we hosted were cutting into his business, I would ask the rest of the audience if this was a common experience. *Are the rest of you also seeing a reduction in business while special events are taking place?*

I was not sarcastic. I did not let disbelief sound in my voice. I made a point of projecting concern. *If this is happening to all of you, we need to know.*

This may sound like a great way to make a bad situation worse, but it works to the presenter's advantage no matter which way it goes.

Most of the time, little or no response comes from the rest of the audience. This unresponsiveness publicly demonstrates that the antagonist is not speaking for the group. The "spokesperson power" he or she was depending on evaporates. The presenter now holds the upper hand and can defer the complaint to a later discussion. *It looks as if this is something you specifically are experiencing. We should get together after this presentation and discuss it further.*

Sometimes, the presenter gets a bonus. The rest of the audience does more than stay quiet; some people start speaking up and disagreeing with the antagonist. They come to the speaker's defense. *I don't know what Bob's problem is; my business is going up.* It is great when this happens! A potential sour point in the presentation turns into a public display of support for the speaker.

Of course, it may go the opposite way. The audience may respond with a chorus of support for the one who spoke out. *Yeah! He's right! We're all losing business during these events!*

It's not a comfortable moment if you are the presenter. You wish you were anywhere but in front of this audience. However, even this audience response will work for you, *if* you manage it correctly.

Think about it. What have you learned? You have learned that there is a widespread concern. Your antagonist *is* speaking for many others. Were you getting anywhere with your proposal? Not really. The audience may have been quiet, but there was a hidden roadblock to your success. At least now you know what it is.

At that point, it is time to take off your presenter's hat and put on your facilitator's hat. *Let's hear what some of the rest of you think. There's no point in my continuing until we work this out.* (Suggestion: Turn off your slides and move in toward the audience as a sign of engagement.)

Are you still in control even though you are not presenting? Yes, you are. You are now the manager of a discussion. It may be a very heated discussion at first, but if you show a willingness to listen and understand, the heat will usually dissipate.

My own experience is that moving the discussion around the room creates a beneficial fluidness to the encounter. It goes from being a potential showdown with one person, to something that I can steer toward the most reasonable voices. Also, I can look for possible transition points back to the presentation. *So the consensus is that the Phase I timetable needs to be more reasonable. Let me show you my proposed Phase II schedule, and see what you think of it.*

Even if the complaint remains unresolved, showing a willingness to listen and discuss it can earn you the audience's tacit approval to continue with your presentation. It helps if you have made a public display of writing it down on a pad or flip chart, assigning it "To Be Resolved" status.

The next time you have an audience member who speaks out against your message, test how much this person speaks for others. It is to your advantage, no matter which way it goes.

Ask for the Identity of "Lots of People"

We just talked about testing a challenger's support. We do this by asking how many others in the room have the same concern.

But what if an antagonist claims support outside the room? This gambit features the telltale phrase "a lot of people," as in "A *lot of people* don't like the changes you are proposing."

Now what do you do? Apparently your challenger is

speaking for legions of people who are not available for questioning.

I call this the mythical-horde-at-the-gate gambit. It reminds me of those old movies that featured a threatening crowd, with pitchforks and torches, just outside the castle gate. In a presentation setting, the disgruntled audience member hopes to put the speaker on the defensive with visions of a similar mob just outside the presentation room.

If this happens to you, fight the temptation to immediately start speaking to whatever issue has been raised. First, ask your challenger to explain who makes up the "lot of people" being referred to. Be politely insistent on this. *When you refer to a "lot of people," who are you specifically referring to?* This is a reasonable question.

At least 90% of the time, your antagonist will backpedal. *Well, I don't know if it's really a lot of people. But I know a couple of people in my department who feel this way!*

Immediately, the mythical horde disappears. You can now graciously, but briefly, speak to the issue or reasonably suggest a meeting later with the concerned few.

In the event your audience member does describe a significant population of dissenters, suggest that a way be found for you to meet with some or all of them. Your audience member may have credibly established that they exist, but that still does not mean he or she can speak for them.

The next time you hear that "a lot of people" do not like what you are presenting, insist on knowing who these people are. Do not accept, without question, that they really exist.

Pull in the Stage Hog

Stage hogs are people who demand attention. They "hog" the stage, determined to have everyone look at them and listen to what they have to say.

Despite their nickname, they do not need a stage. A seat in one of your presentations will do just fine.

They will continuously interrupt you with irrelevant questions and unnecessary comments. Even though you are the official speaker, they will launch into their own monologues. Unrestrained, they will take your presentation off track and bog it down. Then, to add insult to injury, the rest of the audience will ultimately blame you for failing to manage the situation.

Faced with a stage hog, you need to act early and discourage this unproductive competition.

A simple, straightforward management technique is to make the stage hog feel responsible for potentially delaying others in the audience. Assuming that some people need to leave when the presentation is scheduled to end, bring this up as a concern. *We are scheduled to finish up here at three o'clock. I know some of you have other meetings to attend. So that we can finish on time, let me go ahead and get through the rest of my slides. I'll be glad to stay afterward for anyone who wants to discuss the proposal further.*

Most of the time, this simple approach is all that is needed. The stage hog quiets down out of concern for others in the room. He or she was not the least bit concerned about your time needs; however, inconveniencing others in the audience is not good—particularly if some of them are higher ranked.

Unfortunately, some stage hogs are not so easily deterred. You can try to make them concerned for others, but to no avail. They keep right on demanding attention.

When faced with a hard case, you have to do something that is counterintuitive: You have to start pulling this person into your presentation. "But that's crazy!" you say. "I want them out of my presentation, not more involved in it." I know, it *does* sound crazy. But it is wonderfully effective in discouraging stage hog behavior.

If John Doe insists on doing all the talking, to the detriment of your presentation, start asking him to contribute. *John, do you have a different opinion on this?* A couple of minutes later: *I suspect you would handle this different, John. True?* A few minutes later: *What are your thoughts on this, John?*

A rather amazing thing will happen. John—who was determined to be center stage—will now try to get off stage. As you "pull" him in to the presentation, his instinct will be to resist your efforts. Instead of wanting in, he will now want out. He will comment less and even start signaling with his body language that he wants to be left alone (notice the averted eyes, newfound interest in reading the handout, chair pushed back and turned away).

I had to use this technique last year when a gentleman insisted on offering a running commentary on every part of a presentation I was giving. I was part of a program that had a tight schedule involving several other breakout sessions, but this individual clearly did not share my time-management concerns. I tried to get him concerned, but to no avail. So, I started pulling him in. Predictably, the more I requested his commentary the less interested he was in giving it.

A word of warning: Only use this technique when necessary. Even if you use polite, non-threatening language, your stage hog may feel a bit intimidated. Keep this in mind and stop "pulling" as soon as you sense that the other person is retreating.

Also, because of the strong nature of this technique, it is not advisable to use it on people who are in positions of power over you. When they behave as stage hogs, a less direct approach is more appropriate. Learn how this is done in the next segment.

Innocently Quiet the Boss

Bosses are supposed to be supportive. When you present, they should let you have the limelight. If you request some help, fine; otherwise, they should demonstrate to the rest of the audience what appropriate attentiveness looks like. In fact, it's appropriate if they encourage you with an occasional nod of approval.

And so it would be in a perfect world.

Unfortunately, some bosses cannot resist the temptation to take over when a subordinate is presenting. Their reasons are many. Some are self-promoters. Some need to micromanage. Others are chronically insecure and fear someone else getting too much attention. Still others believe that being the main talker is what leadership is all about.

The motives are many, but the result is the same: frustrated subordinates, unsure of what to do, having their status as the main speaker publicly stripped away. It can be demoralizing.

But what can I do? She's my boss!

Many people have had the unhappy experience of a stage hog boss. Ask them what they did about it and they inevitably say they gave up and let the boss have the stage. *What can you do? They have the power.*

Such resignation is understandable. After all, wrestling back control of the presentation could anger the boss. An angry boss is bad news. I had a workshop participant once tell me about a fellow executive who said to the boss: "Excuse me. This is *my* presentation." That fellow's tenure at the company was abruptly cut short.

Fear not; there is a safe way to regain control. Having field tested it with a former boss, I can wholeheartedly attest to its effectiveness.

When faced with a boss who is hogging the stage, wait for an opportunity to speak (they all have to breathe eventually). Then politely tell the boss what is coming up in your presentation and ask if you should show those slides or give more time for the current matter being addressed. In other words, ask the boss how he or she wants to proceed. Ninety-nine percent of the time you will be told to proceed with your presentation. *Go ahead. Show us what you have. We can talk more about this other matter later.*

On the surface, it would appear that you have acknowledged

and acquiesced to your boss' control of the presentation. *Whatever you want, boss; it's up to you.* But, in reality, you have orchestrated the passing of control back to you. You have—dare I use the word—*manipulated* your boss into commanding the very thing you want: the resumption of your presentation. And, you are able to resume because your boss now has to stop talking so you can do what you have been told to do.

Stage hog bosses not only do not get mad when you use this approach, they actually like it. After all, you have provided an opportunity for them to publicly demonstrate their control. You can almost hear them later in their office: "Then I had to tell the guy to get back on track."

Which reminds me to include a warning. You will need good self-esteem to use this technique. You are counting on the boss' ego to help you regain control. Do not let the resulting display of authority bother you. Otherwise, you will subject friends and family to repeated, sarcastic reenactments of the occasion. *Then he says to me, go ahead, go ahead. I'll go ahead him.*

You may be wondering about those times when the boss wants to keep talking and you cannot immediately resume your presentation. You're still in good shape. You acted politely. You delivered a reminder that there is still more to cover. And the others in the room will appreciate your effort.

This defer-to-the-boss technique can be used with any stage hog who is too powerful to confront. For example, you can use it with customers and clients. (They can be even more powerful than your boss.) If you are in a meeting with them, and running out of time to cover everything on the agenda, mention the other items you had planned to cover. Then ask how they feel the remaining time can best be used. Nine out of ten times they will tell you to move on to the other matters. *Oh, please, show us what else you have.*

Defensive Planning

Even though you now know how to react to a stage hog boss, there will be times when you can, and should, prevent the behavior in the first place.

Back in 1999 everyone was talking about Y2K. It was feared that the millennial change was going to create chaos with computers all over the world. Concerned corporations assigned executives exclusively to the task of implementing protective measures.

A few months before the calendar change, I found myself coaching one of these executives. He was getting ready to present his plans to the corporation's executive committee in Europe. His boss, the head of technology, was going to join him.

After he returned from Europe, we met for a debriefing. It was obvious the minute he walked into the room that he was furious. Steam was coming out of his ears. Over the next few minutes he angrily recounted how his boss had hijacked his presentation. He had barely been able to get a word in edgewise as his boss publicly took ownership of his work.

Ironically, on the plane over to Europe, the boss had repeatedly talked about how excited he was that his subordinate—the gentleman I was coaching—was getting such a great opportunity. *I'm so excited for you! This is going to be a career-making opportunity for you to shine in front of the CEO.*

It was not hard to imagine what went through the boss' mind. He obviously took one look at all those senior executives and thought: "Your opportunity? Heck, this is my opportunity!" Unable to resist, he committed presentation grand larceny.

Since the damage was done, I suggested we focus on what to do in the future.

We decided that the best way to keep the boss from stealing a presentation was to give him part of it. In future presentations like the one in Europe, my client would create a few strategic overview slides and then sell his boss on presenting them. *It would be appropriate if you led off by providing the strategic framework—you know, the 30,000-foot view. Then, you can turn it over to me to report on the tactical details.*

Instead of trying to exclude the boss, this approach would more realistically contain the boss. Designating his part as the "big picture overview" effectively reduces his desire to descend into the nitty-gritty details covered in the rest of the presentation.

Don't despair when your boss is a stage hog. Manage from below.

Do Not Fixate on the Distracter

In an ideal audience everyone is politely attentive. With cell phones off, PDAs put away, laptops closed, and conversations finished, they concentrate on nothing but you. Their only movements are approving nods and note taking; their only noise well-placed laughs.

If we could choose what kind of audience behavior we want, this would be our choice every time.

Unfortunately, distracting audience behavior is common. Some people do not know how to be polite listeners; others do not want to be. In a surprising number of companies it is the accepted norm. *Don't mind us; we're just multi-tasking.* Yeah, right.

It would be one thing if it was just annoying. But some of this behavior can be so distracting it threatens your ability to present.

One extreme case I'll never forget featured a middle-aged audience member sticking his tongue out at me. It was bizarre. It was as if I had just tumbled through a time warp and was back in kindergarten. The first couple of times he did it I completely lost my train of thought. I could not believe it was happening.

Another time I was training a group on Wall Street that included a few people addicted to their BlackBerries. All day long they would sneak peeks under the table or under their suit jackets, desperate to see what new messages they had received. Because it was my first encounter with BlackBerry addiction, I was not prepared for how difficult—make that impossible—it was to stop.

In the case of my middle-aged kindergarten student, my

instinct told me his behavior would just get worse if I drew attention to it. And with the BlackBerry addicts I risked creating a bigger distraction if I kept pointing it out. So, in both cases, I had to soldier on despite the distraction.

This requires a healthy dose of willpower.

Poor behavior can pull on your attention like a powerful magnet. Let just one person in the room fall asleep, start playing with a computer, or insist on whispering to others, and you feel compelled to keep looking at them. You fret about their behavior. It distracts you and, to the extent they notice your preoccupation, it distracts others in the audience. Sometimes the only person unaware of the problem is the person causing it.

When you find yourself in a situation like this, make a conscious effort to concentrate on the other people in the audience—the ones who *are* paying attention. Keep reminding yourself that your responsibility is to them. They deserve your attention, not the distracting character.

Obviously, if the behavior is disrupting others in the audience, you have to take steps to stop it. But if it is primarily your distraction, ignore it and actively focus on others. With the case of my kindergarten student, I bypassed him with my eye contact. Out of the corner of my eye I noticed that he eventually gave up when I would not pay attention to him.

The people who *are* paying attention make up your true audience. Reward them with an undistracted, focused presentation performance.

Redirect Personal Attacks.

The Latin term for it is *argumentum ad hominem*—argument against the speaker.

Someone in your audience does not like what you are saying so they take a shot at you. *Doesn't your company have anyone with more experience in this topic?*

Instead of challenging the content of your presentation, they go after you. They try to undermine your message by casting doubt on your qualifications or character. It can be nasty at times.

In part we can thank our political class and media personalities for the popularity of ad hominem arguments. They model the behavior 24/7. It is a simple, cheap way to hurt a political opponent or build news drama. Why work out a thoughtful analysis of another person's proposal when you can just claim that they have dishonest motives or lack credentials. And if it is drama you want, the defensive reaction of the person under attack promises a lively encounter.

If you are ever on the receiving end of an ad hominem argument, DO NOT let yourself get suckered into a personal defense. As soon as you let that happen, you have lost. Remember, the other person is trying to deflect attention from the issues and rattle your cage. You must not let them succeed.

You do not want to fall into a babbling self-defense or launch into an abrasive counterattack—even if it would be satisfying.

Ignore the personal nature of the attack and use the person's own words to flip the attention right back on to the issue(s). If they suggest that you are inexperienced, ask them what they wish you had more experience in. If they declare that you do not know what you are talking about, ask them what it is that they wish you better understood.

You simply do not allow the focus to be put on you. No matter how relentless the other party is, keep redirecting the focus back to the substance of your presentation. This is the best way to neutralize *argumentum ad hominem*. You stay on the high ground, looking professional, and your antagonist's lack of a substantive argument becomes increasingly apparent to the others in the room.

If They Pick on You, Turn into a Hologram

Sometimes the technique of flipping an *ad hominem* argument back on to the issues does not work because the personal attack takes the form of general harassment. It becomes malevolent teasing or "jerking your chain."

I had this experience several years ago when I was asked to train a group of salespeople. Their training department had decided to extend a week of training into Friday afternoon. Normally, these people would have been shuttled to the airport by noon for flights home. But this time someone had the brilliant idea of generating "added value" by making Friday a full day of training with the addition of a three-hour presentation skills workshop.

It would be an understatement to say that these sales reps were not happy. The lucky ones were not going to get home until midnight. The unlucky ones were going to have to wait until Saturday morning to catch a flight. By the time I walked into the room, they were in full obnoxious mode. They were not even trying to be nice. Their luggage was prominently on display right behind their seats, and they were fanning themselves with their plane tickets. I knew I was in trouble when the manager who introduced me practically ran out of the room.

They were on me within minutes. *I noticed you repeatedly move your hands a certain way. Is that the universal hand gesture?*

They took turns trying to jerk my chain. *Excuse me. I hate to break your flow, but I noticed that you move approximately three times per minute. Is that about how much a professional presenter moves?*

I trust you can guess how I wanted to respond. *You want to see a hand gesture? I'll show you a hand gesture. You want to see movement? I'll show you movement.*

But, they were obviously baiting me in hopes that I would fight back. Then it would be 35 to 1 and they could entertain themselves like cats with a mouse. My success depended on not giving them the satisfaction.

I immediately switched into a technique that is sometimes called "fogging." It involves acting like you are in a fog when people are giving you a hard time. In other words, you act like you do not get what is going on or you do not appreciate how upset you should be.

Peter Falk's TV character Columbo was the consummate fogger. Falk played an obsessive police detective who was always being verbally abused by big shots in the community who considered themselves too smart to be caught in their crimes. *Do you always waste people's time like this, Detective Columbo? Maybe you need to buy a dictionary and look up the word alibi.*

Rather than get himself taken off the case by verbally firing back at Mr. Important Person, Columbo would fog. *Sometimes I just get caught up in details. I don't know what it is; I just can't help asking questions until I understand something. It must have something to do with the way I was raised.*

By fogging Columbo made himself into a hologram. When people tried to hurt him with the sticks and stones of their words, they discovered he was not a solid target. Their words passed right through him with no effect.

The sales reps in my workshop experienced the same inability to bother me. When they sarcastically asked about my hand gestures I just offered tips on good hand gesturing. When they commented on how I moved around the room I stressed the importance of moving decisively. *Hmmm. Is that how often I move? Interesting. However often you move, it's important to make sure you stand still for awhile before moving again. That way you avoid aimlessly wandering.*

Eventually the sales reps stopped giving me a hard time. What was the point if I was too dense to get what was going on?

In reality I knew what was going on. I just was not going to give them the satisfaction of taking the bait. In the end, many of them started taking notes and I scored points by finishing in less than three hours. Afterward, I was told that I was the only speaker who had survived that day.

I realize the idea of acting a bit dense might not appeal to you. You would prefer to make it clear to everyone that you know exactly what is going on—and have no intentions of being played for a fool.

Instead, think of yourself as a pro athlete who is refusing to acknowledge the other side's trash talk. Your opponents are trying to rattle you, but you do not even hear what is being said. Instead, you concentrate on scoring with your presentation points. The quality of your presentation is proof enough that you are anything but dense.

Don't Fight

If you don't think you are a good verbal fighter, good. You don't want to be a fighter. When you are the speaker, you cannot win. It is a lose-lose proposition.

Obviously, you lose if an audience member verbally beats you up. But, you also lose if you verbally beat up an audience member. To the others in the room you look like a bully who reacts unprofessionally when provoked.

A class member once told me of a sales executive who proved this axiom. This executive was presenting a new commission structure to a room full of salespeople. The new compensation plan was less generous than the previous one, so the salespeople were angry. They kept challenging aspects of the plan and complaining about the obvious cut in pay. Finally, one salesman stood up and declared: "This isn't fair. I could meet my sales quota and still make less money than last year." This was the last straw for the manager. His response: "I've seen your sales records. If you ever make quota we'll worry about it."

The person telling me the story said that the complaining salesman practically crumbled to the floor. The room went totally quiet and stayed that way for the remainder of the meeting. Afterward, the sales manager had his hands full trying to overcome bad morale and the loss of trust in his leadership. By indulging himself in a public execution he won the battle but potentially lost the war.

The problem is that putting troublemakers in their place feels good. The short-term high is so satisfying it is hard to fight the temptation. We enjoy blowing the smoke off the barrels of our imaginary six guns and slipping them back in their holsters—after mentally spinning them a few times, of course. I'll bet that sales manager's first instinct after leaving that meeting was to brag about how he had "shown them who is boss."

Yes, it feels good, but it does not pay off in the long run. It becomes harder in the future to gain support and build cooperation. Candid discussions that would generate good ideas are less likely. The reputation for being someone who "doesn't take any ____ " comes at a high price. You will always do better in the long run by keeping your cool and responding to antagonism professionally.

Leave the fighting to people on radio and TV talk shows. They create conflict in order to build the size of their audiences. Your success depends on winning audiences by skillfully resolving conflict.